The Washington Reporters

NEWSWORK

The Washington Reporters

STEPHEN HESS

THE BROOKINGS INSTITUTION
Washington, D.C.

Copyright © 1981 by
THE BROOKINGS INSTITUTION
1775 Massachusetts Avenue, N.W., Washington, D.C. 20036

Library of Congress Cataloging in Publication data:

Hess, Stephen.
    The Washington reporters.
    Includes bibliographical references.
    1. Reporters and reporting—Washington, D.C.
    2. Journalists—Washington, D.C.   I. Title.
PN4899.W3H4   070.4'3   80-70077
                                    AACR1

ISBN 0-8157-3594-4
ISBN 0-8157-3593-6 (pbk.)

1 2 3 4 5 6 7 8 9

THE BROOKINGS INSTITUTION is an independent organization devoted to nonpartisan research, education, and publication in economics, government, foreign policy, and the social sciences generally. Its principal purposes are to aid in the development of sound public policies and to promote public understanding of issues of national importance.

The Institution was founded on December 8, 1927, to merge the activities of the Institute for Government Research, founded in 1916, the Institute of Economics, founded in 1922, and the Robert Brookings Graduate School of Economics and Government, founded in 1924.

The Board of Trustees is responsible for the general administration of the Institution, while the immediate direction of the policies, program, and staff is vested in the President, assisted by an advisory committee of the officers and staff. The by-laws of the Institution state: "It is the function of the Trustees to make possible the conduct of scientific research, and publication, under the most favorable conditions, and to safeguard the independence of the research staff in the pursuit of their studies and in the publication of the results of such studies. It is not a part of their function to determine, control, or influence the conduct of particular investigations or the conclusions reached."

The President bears final responsibility for the decision to publish a manuscript as a Brookings book. In reaching his judgment on the competence, accuracy, and objectivity of each study, the President is advised by the director of the appropriate research program and weighs the views of a panel of expert outside readers who report to him in confidence on the quality of the work. Publication of a work signifies that it is deemed a competent treatment worthy of public consideration but does not imply endorsement of conclusions or recommendations.

The Institution maintains its position of neutrality on issues of public policy in order to safeguard the intellectual freedom of the staff. Hence interpretations or conclusions in Brookings publications should be understood to be solely those of the authors and should not be attributed to the Institution, to its trustees, officers, or other staff members, or to the organizations that support its research.

Foreword

IN THE vast literature about how Americans govern themselves, the role of the press is often neglected. Yet the press—no less than the presidency, the judiciary, and the legislature—is a public policy institution and deserves a place in explanations of the governmental process. This book by Stephen Hess, a senior fellow in the Brookings Governmental Studies program, makes a major contribution to the subject with its investigation of the domestic press corps in Washington.

The nation's dependence on the Washington reporters grows in direct proportion to the growth in the size and complexity of the federal government. Their skill largely determines civic knowledge. Who are they? How do they work? How much leeway do they have to choose what they report? Is there anything about their opportunities and constraints that moves the news in certain directions?

Some of the answers are surprising. Even though the media are often thought to be preoccupied with the presidency, for instance, Hess shows how information is channeled through Capitol Hill before it reaches the public— and he suggests that headline writers rather than reporters often give the news a presidential cast. Though economics dominates the news from Washington (along with diplomacy), Hess finds that reporters consider the economics beat so dull that many try to escape from it as soon as they gain enough seniority. He also finds that the Washington press corps is overwhelmingly composed of white males from the Northeast, often trained at highly selective universities, and that home offices exercise far less control over their reporters than the reporters claim. In the final chapter Hess discusses the meaning of his research, including the contention that common traits among reporters— what he calls "the journalist personality"—affect what becomes news.

The author's research was supported by grants from the Ford Foundation and the Earhart Foundation. A great many published materials and recording tapes were provided by the American Enterprise Institute for Public Policy Research, the Nieman Foundation, and the Television News Archive of

Vanderbilt University. The author is grateful to William J. Baroody, Jr.,
James C. Thomson, Jr., and James P. Pilkington of these organizations,
respectively, for making these materials available. He is also grateful for the
continuing interest that Robert B. Goldmann, Fred W. Friendly, and Richard
A. Ware have taken in his research. The following people enriched his
understanding of newswork by their critiques of drafts of this volume: Joseph
Albright, Charles W. Bailey, Robert S. Boyd, Peter Braestrup, David S.
Broder, Peter B. Clark, Julius Duscha, Alan Emory, Andrew Glass, Bernard
Kalb, Marvin Kalb, David Kraslow, H. Finlay Lewis, Norman C. Miller,
Alan L. Otten, Richard Reeves, M. J. Rossant, Charles B. Seib, Eileen
Shanahan, Hugh Sidey, Paul Weaver, Warren Weaver, Jr., James Wieghart,
George F. Will, and Robert Zelnick.

The author thanks his Brookings colleagues Martha Derthick, Herbert
Kaufman, A. James Reichley, Gilbert Y. Steiner, and James L. Sundquist
for comments on the research design and chapter drafts; Radmila Nikolić and
Donna D. Verdier for administrative support; Diane Hammond for editorial
services; and Diana Regenthal for preparing the index.

Christine C. de Fontenay served as statistical consultant and director of
the computer work for the project. David A. Padgett was her principal
associate on the programming work. The other members of her staff were Pat
Bruner, James Altman, Janet Braun, and June Smith. Jill S. Ehrenreich
prepared the list of reporters for the survey. Elaine Meyer was consulted on
survey design. Amy B. McIntosh, Helen Graham, Richard V. Nalley, Jeffrey
Rayport, Diana Charnov, and Melissa Cook did the telephone interviewing
and coded the stories.

All the views expressed in this book, of course, are those of the author and
should not be ascribed to the Ford Foundation, to the Earhart Foundation,
or to the trustees, officers, or other staff members of the Brookings Institution.

BRUCE K. MACLAURY
President

January 1981
Washington, D.C.

For Jane and Alan

Author's Note

OVER HALF of the 1,250 Washington reporters who cover national government for U.S. commercial news outlets contributed their time for this study. The generosity of these men and women makes this book possible.

The first stage of the project in 1977 consisted of 150 interviews. These usually lasted from one to two hours. Almost a third were with bureau chiefs, who were asked how their staff resources were allocated and organized to report on the activities of government. Other interviewees were chosen because of their long history in Washington journalism or because they were known to have special knowledge of different types of news operations or beats. A limited number of news executives in six cities were also interviewed in order to try to gather some home-office perspectives on how Washington bureaus fitted into the parent organizations. A 150-page summary of hunches—called a "state-of-the-project report"—was then distributed to a diverse group of journalists for comments. (These people are acknowledged in the foreword.)

In stage two of the investigation, 1978, a questionnaire was designed, tested, and revised. Calls to all news operations listed in *Hudson's Washington News Media Contacts Directory* and the *Congressional Directory* produced the list of 1,250 reporters. All were mailed questionnaires and 292 usable responses were returned. Respondents were assured anonymity.

Fourteen pages of the sixteen-page questionnaire were in the form of a daily log, a technique sometimes used in surveys of television viewing. For each day of a single week, reporters were asked to note the stories they were working on, who initiated them, how many persons were interviewed, whether interviews were on or off the record, how many of the interviews were with press secretaries or other government public information officers, what types of events were attended, what documents were used, and other very specific questions relating to the work of the day. While this elaborate format undoubtedly discouraged participation in the project, the responses it produced were of an unusually high quality. Reporters have complained of the very broad and general questions in some past surveys; they seemed much more comfortable when asked for precise information about their current work.

Another questionnaire, also prepared in 1978, was administered by telephone. Reporters were called at random, but because respondents to the mail questionnaire had indicated their type of employer (wire service, television network, and so forth), it was possible to adjust the telephone sample so that telephone-plus-mail-questionnaires would accurately reflect the relative sizes of the various components that make up the Washington press corps. The telephone survey yielded 194 usable responses. Both mail and telephone questionnaires requested the same information about the reporters' backgrounds—age, sex, race, where they lived during childhood, the number of years they spent in school, the colleges they attended, the degrees they obtained, and their fields of study. These data constituted a file that represented 38 percent of all Washington reporters. (In ten cases where exactly the same information came from the mail and telephone surveys, the responses, obviously having come from the same source, were tabulated only once.) In the telephone survey the reporters were also asked to explain their views on matters that could best be handled as open-ended questions, such as political bias in the press corps, pack journalism, consumer and home-office reactions to their stories, attribution of sources, breaking news, and job and assignment preferences. It was possible to devise codes that translated the answers to some of the open-ended questions into numbers and percentages; otherwise, the information was used in narrative form. Since by far the largest group of Washington reporters—nearly 40 percent—works for newspapers, this group becomes the focus of this part of the study.

The final stage of the project was devoted to analyzing a week of Washington stories appearing in April 1978 in twenty-two newspapers, on the weeknight news programs of the three television networks, and in a weekly newsmagazine. The intent was to describe what comes out of Washington news gathering, just as the reporters' logs elicited what goes in. (The weeks, however, were not the same.) All told, 2,022 stories were coded. The data gathered for each story included headline, by-line, length, placement, the coverage of various institutions and topics, persons quoted or otherwise mentioned, documents referred to, whether the story was meant to be an interpretation of news, and—for newspapers—whether the story was regional or had a regional angle.

Whenever appropriate, various other data were also recorded: the relative weight that a story gave to the presidency and the Congress; the level of congressional action (from the introduction of legislation through Senate-House conference committee deliberation), and types of congressional hearing. The place of origin of the front-page lead stories was tabulated so as to judge the importance of Washington news vis-à-vis news from other places.

Two other, subordinate, surveys were conducted. The first involved a questionnaire sent to a number of independent writers on national affairs, chosen because each had once been a full-time Washington reporter, that sought to understand why they had exchanged one kind of journalism for another. In the second, conducted when the *New York Times* was on strike in 1978, chiefs of major bureaus were asked what effect the absence of the *Times* had on their operations—an oblique way of attempting to define the role of a publication that many consider to be a reference point for national news gatherers.

The results of these interviews, surveys, tabulations, and cross-tabulations depict Washington newswork at a specific moment late in the twentieth century. The percentages presented here will not stand still, of course, but some conditions that can be identified through examining contemporary behavior shift slowly indeed. In the mid-1930s, before nuclear weapons and television, Leo C. Rosten, then a graduate student at the University of Chicago, wrote an account of the world of the Washington correspondent that still tells us a great deal about why news is as it is. Perhaps after some periods of social or technological revolution the future is no longer much like the past. But such periods do not come often. Despite recurring predictions, the press is not now at such a disjuncture.

The Washington Reporters is the first of several books I hope to write about the press in the United States under the collective title of *Newswork*. The need is to explain how the press fits into the web of governance, and to create research tools and a body of data for others to use in future investigations. The memoirs of journalists, while often valuable as pieces of history, are designed for other purposes. Schools of journalism or communication are primarily centers of training, not research. Departments of political science or government seem to have a long-standing bias against this area of inquiry. Too bad. Journalists are great fun to study.

S.H.

Contents

CHAPTER ONE

𝔚𝔬𝔯𝔨

To LISTEN to many Washington reporters talk about work is to imagine the beleaguered band at the Alamo. They are surrounded by editors who do not understand their problems, by deadlines that are unrealistic and assignments that are simplistic, by politicians who are manipulative and bureaucrats who are uncommunicative and consumers who are either uninterested or cranks. They are employed by penny-pinching organizations that will not let them travel to the places where news is being made. They are never given the space or time to do justice to their stories. They are constantly being badgered by silly requests from the home office. The odds against their being able to do their jobs are horrendous.

I have a hell of a fight with [my editor] over the "trivialization" of news. Editors are getting fed up with serious institutional problems, with articles on what government should and shouldn't do. It took me a week to get an article in the paper on government reorganization, then [the editor] attacked it as "another story of government glop." . . . Editors feel they aren't doing their job if they don't screw around with your copy. . . . The power center [of my organization] is New York. But it's a zero news town. We have to call New York before we can go to the bathroom. . . . I get a lot of letters from guys who want to know if I'm married, personal comments about my clothes and hair. Or they ask me "Dear Abby" questions about their lives. I get little about the news I cover. . . . Usually I get letters from far-out people who see communists under every hat. . . . We're being used by publicity-seeking members of Congress. . . . Reporters are suspicious of bureaucrats; we consider them always ready to hide behind regulations, unbending paper-shufflers. . . . This is a company town, let's face it. So it's inevitable that they control the news to some extent.[1]

Is this really the world of the Washington reporter? Or are these tales spun

---

1. Ellipses separate words of one speaker from those of another.

to feed a love of complaining? To intensify the pleasures of a difficult job? To create a specialness of us against them? "We complain because we are quasi-creative workers," contends Albert Hunt of the *Wall Street Journal.* Creative people are supposed to complain. But in contrast to the often amusing, sometimes bitter, comments of reporters, there are more careful ways to calculate job satisfaction, the extent of disagreements with employers, hours worked, travel, who initiates stories, the amount of copy editing, and story placement. When 38 percent of the Washington reporters who cover national government for the American commercial media answered elaborate questionnaires in 1978, their responses portrayed a very different world.[2]

ALL SELF-RESPECTING reporters are capable of pleasurably recounting the wrongs committed against them by their editors or producers and by politicians or public officials. But when asked whether they are happy in their work, the overwhelming majority, 84 percent, rate themselves as satisfied. (Forty percent are very satisfied, 44 percent fairly satisfied, 14 percent somewhat dissatisfied, and only 2 percent very dissatisfied.)

Prestige beats usually rate high in satisfaction, among them politics, science, the White House, and diplomacy. Low-satisfaction assignments include regional news, the Supreme Court, regulatory agencies, and domestic departments. Specialized publications, television networks, and magazines have the greatest percentages of satisfied reporters, though reporters for specialized publications do not rate themselves "very" satisfied.

Reporters on influential outlets are not more content as a group than those who work for the noninfluentials. Anecdotally, at least, most tensions in Washington journalism are in the premier organizations. Good gossip, of course, is always the tales told of kings—the ups and downs of famous names at a television network or a major newspaper are intrinsically interesting. Yet the anecdotal evidence of high tension suggests reasons why job satisfaction is not higher at the places where the prestige is greatest: Washington news,

2. Arthur Ochs Sulzberger, the publisher of the *New York Times*, once told an audience, "Let me pass along a tip on how to detect bias in any speeches on this subject: If he talks about 'the media' he's against us; if he talks about 'the press' he's for us." See "Business and the Press: Is the Press Anti-Business?" *Vital Speeches*, May 1, 1977, p. 426. This study uses *the press* and *the media* interchangeably, one hopes without prejudice. However, at the outset it should be noted that this is *not* a book about foreign correspondents in Washington, the local Washington media (other than those on the national desks of the *Washington Post* and the *Washington Star*), those who are exclusively news processors (editors, producers), full-time columnists, reporters who do not cover national government, or the noncommercial media (other than the Associated Press, a cooperative, and two church-affiliated newspapers, the *Christian Science Monitor* and the *Deseret News*). For a discussion of the parameters of this survey, see Author's Note.

being more important in these organizations, is more worth fighting about; and since these organizations are national, and therefore more centrally controlled, reporters have less autonomy. (The power plays at little-known publications may be equally fierce, merely less noticed. Smaller organizations are probably not composed of "nicer" people; they just fight on other grounds—and less in the public eye.)

Specialists are considerably more satisfied than generalists; the older the reporters, the more likely they are satisfied (although there is a slight rise in the dissatisfaction rating for reporters in their forties); conservatives are more satisfied than liberals; there are no job satisfaction differences between men and women.

When Washington reporters are given a list of ten types of disagreements and asked to rate how often they have these disagreements with their home offices (0 = never, 1 = seldom, 2 = sometimes, 3 = often), the overall average disagreement rating is 0.92, or slightly less than seldom. Constant combat is not characteristic of relations between reporters and editors; benign neglect is a better description. For most journalists in Washington, the home office is far away and out of sight. Local editors are consumed with other problems, and their Washington reporters are too experienced to require close supervision and too knowledgeable—even intimidating—to have their judgments overruled. Local editors fume a lot about the Washington staff not knowing what "the people" really want, but rarely try to run the Washington bureau from headquarters. (In those cases where Washington is headquarters, this obviously does not apply.)

Given the overall low level of disagreement, the most revealing information gleaned from this question is what reporters and their bosses do fight about. The majority of arguments—56 percent—concerns matters that could be called professional: length of the story, its placement in the publication or broadcast, the time to write, and writing style—in descending order of importance to the reporters.[3]

Although a few reporters contend that the Washington press corps suffers

3. A *Washington Post* reporter talks of a colleague "who gets pissed off if one word is changed," but he says this attitude is rare. "You survive by never reading your story in the paper." Reporters who have the most disagreements over style are those on the diplomatic, Supreme Court, science, regulatory agency, and economics beats, who must translate technical information into lay language. The only other area registering above average style disagreements is the routine general assignments, often given to young reporters, whose problem is inexperience. As the press corps becomes more "educated," more new reporters may have trouble with their editors over style. As one television network correspondent put it, "I was used to an academic writing style."

from verbosity and that editors' efforts to limit the length of stories is a good thing, nearly a fifth of all fights are about the length of stories. As a top newspaper reporter muses, "What do people fight over . . . money? . . . sex? In journalism the territorial imperative is space."

There is a widely held belief among newspaper reporters that the space devoted to nonadvertising—the news hole—is shrinking.[4] Whether this is true or not, there are other changes that affect how much space each reporter can expect. Page makeup has changed (bigger headlines, more white space, larger photographs, more indexes). And competition from both Washington and non-Washington material is greater (more sports coverage and service features, business market listings, even fiction; larger Washington bureau staffs; more stories from wire services, supplemental news services, syndicates, and free-lancers).

When the television networks doubled the length of their evening news programs in 1963 they added stories rather than lengthened them. Although the chief executive of one network news division, interviewed in 1977, predicted that another doubling of broadcast time would mean longer stories, the nature of the medium makes this problematical—listeners cannot skip items that bore them, as readers can, and bored listeners may turn off their sets or, worse, turn to another channel.

At the same time, Washington reporters say their stories need even more time or space. The federal government makes more news: it is bigger, more complex, and it is assuming more functions in society. Changes in law and in congressional rules make more information available. The definition of news is expanding, as fewer topics are now considered off limits to public comment. Furthermore, in newspaper journalism a form of anecdotal writing (pioneered at the *Wall Street Journal*), which cannot be easily compressed, is gaining in popularity.

The other significant category of disagreements—nearly a third—has to do with autonomy, the reporter resisting home-office requests, assignments,

---

4. Advertising space in daily newspapers rose from 59 percent in 1947 to 62 percent in 1955. See Fritz Machlup, *The Production and Distribution of Knowledge in the United States* (Princeton University Press, 1962), p. 228. On the other hand, Lee Dirks, special assistant to the publisher of the *Detroit Free Press*, says that his study of twenty-nine newspapers in the thirteen largest urban areas shows news content rose 18 percent (daily) and 6 percent (Sunday) from 1965 through 1974. Leo Bogart, executive vice president of the Newspaper Advertising Bureau, responds that "total number of pages have continued to increase with increased advertising. As that happens you get a larger news content but a declining percentage of the total paper. So [on the question of the shrinking news hole] you can interpret it both ways." See conference transcript, "What is the Future of Big City Newspapers?" Woodrow Wilson International Center for Scholars, Washington, D.C., January 19, 1977.

or story angles. "An editor says this should be the lead and I say that's the lead. I want to do it my way." Autonomy causes the greatest conflict in prestigious organizations (which have greater leverage over their reporters) and among prestigious reporters (who expect the most autonomy). This explains, perhaps, the exit from daily journalism of such luminaries as David Halberstam, Tom Wolfe, and Gay Talese. The late Laurence Stern, an editor of the *Washington Post*, was fond of saying, "When the history of the newspaper business is written, it will be about those who left it." Although one might expect that friction over autonomy would be much more prevalent in network television, where high technology increases organizational control at the same time that the star system increases reporters' demands, this is not so. (Those working for network television are only slightly above the average for all reporters.) What may dampen conflict in this medium is that unhappy correspondents can sell their services to only a limited number of networks. (The most autonomous journalist, then, would be a prestigious reporter working for a nonprestigious outlet, such as the late Peter Lisagor of the *Chicago Daily News*.)

Fights over money—for travel and expenses—are modest. Also, only 4 percent say they ever argue with their editors over politics—the political slant that the home office or the reporter may wish to give a story. This is a major change since 1936, when Leo Rosten asked Washington reporters whether they had "had stories played down, cut, or killed for 'policy' reasons" and 56 percent said *yes*. William Rivers, asking the same questions in 1961, found that 7 percent answered in the affirmative.[5] But by 1978, writing to fit the editorial positions of publishers had simply disappeared as an issue for contention. While it is possible that this is because publishers and reporters now agree, the evidence is otherwise: many reporters make a point of noting that they do not share the political ideologies of their publications. The near absence of disagreements over political slant is a by-product of higher professional standards as well as the passing of the press "lords"—the Robert R. McCormicks and William Randolph Hearsts—publishers of strong political opinions (and sometimes strong political ambitions), who viewed their publications as outlets for their own views. Many have been succeeded by chain operations, which accept "objectivity" as a necessity of doing business in diverse communities, and by the electronic media, which are legally mandated to be "fair."

5. Leo C. Rosten, *The Washington Correspondents* (1937; reprint ed., Arno Press, 1974), p. 352; William L. Rivers, "The Correspondents after 25 Years," *Columbia Journalism Review*, vol. 1 (Spring 1962), p. 5.

Disagreements with the home office are greater in broadcast journalism than in print, about both story length and assignments. Money for travel and expenses is more of an issue at small operations, such as local television stations and regional news services. Fights over story angle and political slant most often occur at magazines, which interpret the news. Specialized publications record the fewest disagreements. However, the range of disagreements does not differ very much among the various types of news organizations.

Nor is there much variation by beat, except for the Supreme Court beat, which is above average in every disagreement category. Reporters on almost all beats are unhappy about story length, with White House reporters being unhappiest. Class A general assignment reporters have the most disagreements about story placement; White House reporters, about time to write; and class B general assignment reporters, about home-office requests. (For the purposes of this study, general assignment reporters are divided into two categories: the class A general assignment reporter, a senior person, even the bureau chief, picks his or her own stories; the class B general assignment reporter, often a younger person, is sent on a daily basis to those events that may produce news outside the main flow.)

Generalists have more disagreements than specialists; the older the reporter, the fewer the disagreements; there are no differences in the disagreement ratings of women and men; conservative reporters have fewer disagreements with their home-office editors than do liberal reporters, in light of the ten disagreement categories. The few blacks in the study claim to have few disagreements.

The low level of disagreements between Washington reporters and their home offices need not be because the reporters have been housebroken—sociologists make much of newsroom "socialization"[6]—but because they so often get their way. It is not necessary to push against an open door. A method of measuring reporters' autonomy is to ask "who was primarily responsible for initiating" their latest stories. In 856 cases, reporters initiated their own stories 69 percent of the time, home offices initiated 11 percent, and bureau chiefs, 10 percent. Only the lowest reporters on the totem pole, those covering class B general assignments, initiate less than a majority of their stories (44 percent). Otherwise, there are no beats on which reporters

---

6. The pioneering work in this area is Warren Breed, "Social Control in the Newsroom: A Functional Analysis," *Social Forces*, vol. 33 (May 1955), pp. 326–35.

claim that their home offices generate as much as 16 percent of the stories or that the bureau chiefs generate as much as 18 percent.[7]

The editor of a chain newspaper in a western state is highly critical of his operation's Washington bureau. His complaints are unusual in that he does not fault the staff for failing to relate to his community but rather for lacking enterprise. Looking over the Washington schedule of the day before, he asks, "Is there any story here that couldn't have been written in three hours?" He thinks not. He has lots of ideas about stories that should be written, yet he says he never makes requests and does not offer suggestions at the chain's annual meeting of editors.

The editor of a chain newspaper in a southern state is also critical of the stories he gets from Washington, but his is the more typical comment, that Washington reporters have lost touch with the rest of the country. (Unlike the western editor, he runs a high percentage of the copy he receives.) He, too, does not make his views known to the Washington office. "[The bureau chief] would say I'm very poor about generating ideas, but it's ninety out of a hundred on my list of priorities."

Being very busy is not the only reason that editors give their Washington reporters so much freedom. Editors who have not had Washington experience often seem to hold their Washington reporters in awe ("Who am I to tell them what to write?"). And editors who have had Washington experience often agree with the views of their Washington bureaus.

Nor are Washington reporters very closely supervised by their bureau chiefs, at least in the matter of story assignments. Says the bureau chief of a large independent newspaper, "Reporters generate 65 percent of spot stories . . . and some beats generate up to 85 percent of the stories, such as the State Department." He explains, "Most reporters do a much better job if they generate their own stories. They're the ones who really know what's going on." This may be true, but it also avoids hassles. Most bureau chiefs are themselves reporters or columnists; supervising a staff is not high on their list of satisfactions.

Autonomy is very different at the more highly centralized television networks and weekly newsmagazines. Network correspondents claim to initiate only half of their stories. Nearly 22 percent of the assignments come from their bureau chiefs, who are not burdened with their own writing as

7. Chain bureau reporters in Washington initiate 7 percent more of their own stories than reporters who work for independent papers and get 5 percent fewer assignments from their papers' home offices.

they are on newspapers. Magazine reporters say they initiate 57 percent of their stories. Since television networks and newsmagazines are counted among the influentials of journalism, these reporters, it might appear, have chosen to exchange autonomy for other rewards. The reverse exchange could be said to be the case of top journalists who work for less illustrious operations. But, of course, the play of fortuity is such that few reporters are actually presented with this choice. Moreover, it is instructive to note that the Washington reporters of such tightly controlled organizations as *Time* and the Columbia Broadcasting System do at least as many stories of their own initiation as stories thought up by others.

The notion that "editors feel they aren't doing their job if they don't screw around with your copy" was also tested. The replies of reporters, who were asked to indicate "how much editing was done by the home office" on 473 of their stories, suggest a gap between complaint and practice. Over half the stories (51 percent) are not edited at all; and the editing is minor on nearly all the rest. Only 3 percent of the stories are substantially edited.

The amount of editing relates importantly to the type of news organization. Television network news can be thought of as preedited—carefully constructed to fit time segments before it goes to New York. Network correspondents report that there is no home-office editing 93 percent of the time, minor editing 7 percent of the time. In magazine writing, on the other hand, the home office is expected to play a more significant role, and here some editing is reported 62 percent of the time. "It's a myth," says a newsmagazine editor, "that reporters file beautiful, finished copy that the editors then butcher." Newspapers fall between television and magazines on the editing scale.

What is most important in gauging the freedom of Washington reporters from home-office control is how few respondents—even those who work for magazines—indicate that their work is substantially edited; no stories of regional news service reporters and radio reporters are substantially edited. How much editing is done relates most to the age of the reporter, the youngest being the most edited.[8] Only one of the substantially edited stories is from a high-prestige beat, but this too is age-related, since these are the places where young reporters are seldom located.

In terms of the placement of stories, a bureau chief says, "Our papers understand that we represent an investment. The return on the investment

8. For example, 35 percent of reporters aged twenty through twenty-nine say that their copy receives no editing; 60 percent, minor editing; and 5 percent, substantial editing. At the other end of the age spectrum, 69 percent of reporters aged fifty and over claim no editing; 31 percent, minor editing; and none of them are substantially edited.

is the stories we do. They want to give us good treatment." When Washington reporters were asked to indicate placement of 561 major stories that they had just written, 51 percent rate them "prominent" (for television networks, this means the stories appeared on the evening news), 48 percent get "secondary" treatment, and 1 percent are not used. Above-average display of stories is registered by reporters for television networks, radio, and chain newspaper bureaus. The figures for influential and noninfluential outlets are about the same. Class A general assignment reporters have the highest percentage of prominently placed stories, and those on the regulatory agencies beat, the lowest. Nearly 18 percent of the newspaper stories are on the front page.

Among the reasons for not using stories: a newspaper catering to the business community kills a piece because its rival has the story first; a magazine reporter sets out to show that a government project is "excessively costly and way behind schedule," but I "couldn't quite prove it." A completed story, however, almost always turns up in print or on the air.

Stories by reporters on high-prestige beats, as expected, are more prominently displayed and less edited. These reporters initiate somewhat fewer stories than their colleagues on the low-prestige beats, reflecting, possibly, bureau chiefs' and home-office editors' interest in the coverage of major events and institutions. Reporters appear to pay a slight price in independence for assignment to the beats that are most important to their supervisors.

THUS we find that an overwhelming percentage of Washington reporters are satisfied in their work, seldom have disagreements with their home offices, and initiate most of their own stories; home-office editing of their copy is usually nonexistent or minor, and a majority of their stories receive prominent placement. There are other pleasurable facets of a Washington reporter's life: they do not work excessively long hours, their jobs require only a modest amount of routine office work, and, as help-wanted ads might put it, there are good opportunities for travel.

The reporters who kept complete logs of their activities for a week average forty-two hours on the job. Only 33 of 237 reporters work more than fifty hours for their employer. Television network correspondents average forty-five hours a week. There is virtually no difference in the workweeks of those employed by independent and chain newspapers, but reporters on the influential outlets work about five hours longer than the others.

Reporters' schedules can be widely erratic. There are times of crisis and periods of intense labor, such as the end of a congressional session, a decision week at the Supreme Court, and trips with presidents, secretaries of state, or candidates. But in a period picked for its ordinariness, with no unusual events going on, Washington reporters are not found to be overtaxed. Indeed, their considerable free-lance activities (27 percent of the press corps) attest to the time available for other pursuits.

Washington reporters average less than two hours a week on typing letters and clerical chores. Twenty-one percent say that they spend none of their time on such activities, 38 percent spend one hour a week. "I avoid it at all costs," says a writer on a specialized publication. "I throw out a lot of stuff instead of filing," says a newspaper reporter. Reporters get few letters that demand replies and have no special government regulations to comply with in triplicate. They work alone or in small units, negating most need for most interoffice memos, which do not fit the hurry-up nature of journalism, anyway. An occasional reporter objects to the lack of secretarial help ("I have to sweet-talk a secretary into doing my typing when I have to send a letter that must look neat"). But most prefer, and take pride in, journalism's nonbureaucratic traditions. The absence of paperwork distinguishes reporting from other professional or managerial jobs of comparable status.

"This is the most traveled press corps in the world," says a newspaper reporter of eighteen years' experience, nine in Washington. On average, he is probably correct: the figure works out to nineteen days a year for each reporter. But time away from Washington on assignment is unequally divided: television network correspondents average forty days, wire service and specialized publications reporters are away less than seven days. The big travelers cover diplomacy (forty-eight days), class A general assignments (forty-seven days), and the White House (thirty-two days). At the other extreme are the reporters assigned to the Supreme Court (ten days) and energy (nine days). Travel is also closely correlated with age. Of reporters in their twenties, almost half have no out-of-Washington assignments; most reporters fifty years old and older spend fifteen to thirty days away; the big travelers—over thirty days—are reporters in their middle years, especially those in their thirties. Women take short trips, men are away longer. Reporters on the influentials do a great deal more traveling than reporters on the noninfluentials. Three percent of the newspaper stories and 6 percent of the television stories by Washington correspondents are filed from places outside of the capital.

SOME of the pleasures of Washington reporting are generic to journalism—minimal routine office work, for example. Some satisfactions derive from being far from the home office—such as little editorial supervision. Other satisfactions come from covering the nation's capital—being eyewitness to important events. And there are satisfactions that are a product of having achieved prominence in the profession, including exotic travel. Yet there are also special problems and stresses that are part of newswork in Washington.

The reporters' isolation from their consumers and their organizations is often considerable. For some, this lack of connection is the dark side of freedom. It can make the workplace a little more unsettling. A fourth of Washington reporters receive no letters or calls from readers or listeners: wire service and radio reporters almost never hear from their consumers; two-thirds of the press corps get three or fewer letters or phone calls in a week. "I consider more than six letters a month a landslide," says a member of a chain bureau. Of those in the mass media, only television network correspondents get an appreciable response from their audience.[9]

"The public is very supine" except on a few highly emotional issues, such as abortion and the Equal Rights Amendment, and this mail is often generated by organized groups. In general, reporters give low marks to their letter writers. "We get some pretty bizarre reactions, especially the reporter covering psychology" (from a specialized news service); "half are from crackpots, a lot from convicts saying their rights are being violated on something" (from a chain newspaper bureau); "some want pictures" (from a television network); "I get a lot from John Birchers and Ku Kluxers" (from an influential newspaper). Mail that expresses an opinion of the reporters' work tends to be heavily unfavorable, particularly of those covering diplomacy.[10] Only journalists on specialized publications, and a few specialists at other news outlets, get mostly favorable reactions; they talk of a sense of community with their consumers.[11]

Says a radio reporter, "It doesn't bother me not hearing from listeners. I realize I'm just a voice. However, I hate getting no feedback from my organization. This lack of guidance is terribly frustrating." Fifteen percent of all Washington reporters claim that they receive no home-office reaction to their stories. Another 46 percent characterize the response as minor. Only

9. Sixty percent of television network correspondents say they receive more than four letters a week, a third get over thirteen.

10. Reporters describe their mail as 20 percent favorable and 29 percent unfavorable; 18 percent merely requests information. The ratio for newspapers is three unfavorable letters to every favorable one; for television networks, two unfavorable to one favorable.

11. At specialized publications, 49 percent of the reporters get over four letters a week; 27 percent getting more than thirteen letters. The mail is two to one favorable.

those who work for television networks and specialized publications say that they get substantial reaction from their home offices.[12]

"There's no systematic feedback, no memos or notes," says a reporter on a large independent newspaper. "That's fine with me. The less feedback the better." Yet the radio reporter says, "This lack of guidance is terribly frustrating." Which is the prevailing view? The answer relates partly to age. A twenty-four-year-old specialized publication writer says, "There's not enough feedback for me." On the other hand, a sixty-nine-year-old newspaper reporter contends, "I seldom surprise them, they don't surprise me. There's no need to pass reactions back and forth." Another pattern seems to be that those who do not hear regularly complain of no feedback and those who get substantial home-office reaction complain of interference.

The isolation of reporters from both consumers and the management of their own organizations contributes to their seeking rewards from association with (and their standing among) their colleagues. Recalling his days on the *New York Times*, sociologist Robert Darnton says, "We really wrote for one another. Our primary reference group was spread around us in the newsroom."[13] Yet those who claim they receive considerable reaction to their work from their home offices rate themselves more satisfied with their jobs, and, conversely, those getting only minor reaction from headquarters are less satisfied. (And as noted, there is no correlation between a high number of disagreements with the home office and low job satisfaction.) Moreover, reporters who get more feedback from their editors give their bureaus a higher rating for "informing the public." These findings are difficult to reconcile with the traditional view of autonomy-seeking reporters and with their self-image as unreconstructed individualists. The feeling that their work is being carefully scrutinized turns out to be more important to reporters than they choose to admit.

Isolated from consumer and home office, Washington journalists feel themselves increasingly out of touch with the nation. Asked to comment on a cluster of statements—"Reporters often miss how government affects people 'out there' " and "Washington reporters have lost touch with their roots"— 82 percent of the news corps agree, and 54 percent think the problem is serious.

---

12. Half of television network reporters and 46 percent at specialized publications say that home-office feedback is "substantial," although, it should be noted, Washington is the home office of many of the specialized operations.

13. Robert Darnton, "Writing News and Telling Stories," *Daedalus*, vol. 104 (Spring 1975), p. 176.

Radio and newspaper reporters are the most concerned; wire service and magazine reporters are most likely to see no problem. Views differ depending on which end of Pennsylvania Avenue the reporter is located: at the White House, 88 percent of the reporters believe the problem is serious, while the percentage drops to 40 among congressional reporters on Capitol Hill. Almost all black reporters say that the Washington news corps is out of touch; women more than men are apt to call this a serious problem; reporters for the influential outlets are less likely than those on the noninfluentials to see a problem here; and reporters fifty years old and over are least likely to worry about being out of touch.

There is a relationship between reporters saying that they are out of touch with the rest of the country and the degree to which they fraternize with their own kind in Washington. Almost half of reporters' closest friends in Washington are other journalists.[14] Among their nonjournalist friends, at least 55 percent are in government or government-related fields, such as lobbying and political party work. The older the reporter (which assumes a longer working life in Washington), the more likely his or her close friends are other Washington reporters: by the time Washington reporters reach fifty years of age, nearly two-thirds of their closest Washington friends are journalists.[15] Those in broadcast journalism (radio and network television) are most likely to have friends in the news media. Reporters on beats centered in newsrooms and press galleries (Congress, White House, State Department) tend to have more reporter friends than those on beats without a central location (regulatory agencies, economics, science). Reporters who say that none of their closest friends are journalists think the press corps is more out of touch than those who say that their three closest friends are in journalism.

What can be done to close the gap between Washington reporters and the rest of the country? Travel, say reporters. Eighty-one percent of the press corps think they should have the opportunity to spend more time away from Washington. "Drive across the country," advises a newsmagazine reporter. "I did it in sixty-seven. Nobody believed me afterwards when I said LBJ wouldn't be reelected." A newspaper reporter in a chain bureau says, "I make

14. Reporters were asked how many of their three closest friends in Washington are journalists. The mean score is 1.4, with 1.5 representing half.

15. For reporters in the twenty through twenty-nine-year age bracket, an average of 1.27 of their three closest friends in Washington are other Washington journalists; for ages thirty through thirty-nine, the average is 1.33; for ages forty through forty-nine, 1.42; and for ages fifty and over, 1.82. Blacks and women, tending to be younger, have fewer reporter friends than whites and males. But the fact that black reporters list fewer of their closest friends in the press corps probably also reflects the scarcity of black reporters.

it a point to travel back to Ohio for extended trips of several weeks, at least twice or three times a year. It almost always improves my perspective on how to treat news out of Washington." The reporters who do the most traveling are the most convinced there is a problem.[16]

The press corps is almost equally divided over whether rotating reporters between Washington and the home office would be a workable solution to the problem of losing touch with consumers. (Fifty-two percent say *yes*, 48 percent say *no*.) Many mention one newspaper that keeps its reporters in Washington for only a few years and, as a result, has lost some of its best people. Sixty-two percent believe that rotation would cause serious staff losses, ranging from 71 percent on magazines down to 54 percent at wire services. "You'd have an armed revolt on your hands," says a newspaper chain reporter.

Arguments against rotation usually revolve around acquired knowledge. "Washington is the kind of city where experience pays off." "Contacts are very important, so it doesn't make sense for a paper to shift reporters around too often." "It's a bloody waste to send someone out to the boondocks after he has learned to cover this city." Of course Washington reporters are hardly the ones to offer a disinterested opinion. "I don't want to live in Baltimore." "Reporters going back to local papers would have to take a huge pay cut." "We can't go back to covering cops and robbers." "It would be hard to move with husband and wife both working in Washington."

On the other hand, there are Washington journalists who believe "it's dangerous to have a reporter here longer than most of the politicians" and "rotation holds out hope for other reporters back home." Others point to existing policies of rotating foreign correspondents that, although on a much smaller scale, have not caused problems. "There'd be a lot of bitching and moaning," says a network correspondent, "but there's so large a supply of reporters that filling the ranks in Washington is not a problem." Rotation, however, would be a messy, unpleasant policy to put into practice, and organizations do not do things that are messy and unpleasant unless forced to by necessity.

COVERING Washington would be as difficult as "trying to nail currant jelly to the wall" (a phrase Theodore Roosevelt used in another context) if the

16. Journalists are quick to point out that being separated from the country "is a problem of government, too" (from a magazine reporter) or "reporters lose touch just as do members of Congress" (from a television network reporter). A wire service man says, "Reporters anywhere are out of touch. Even when I was in North Carolina, I didn't focus on roads and schools, which people really care about. I wrote about ERA, which is what I cared about."

canvas—massive in size, complicated in detail, ambiguous in intention—
were not simplified and reduced by agreements on what is newsworthy. News,
for most reporters, is (a) a tangible activity—a congressional vote, a Supreme
Court decision, a presidential speech—that (b) occurs in the current twenty-
four-hour period. Thus three-quarters of Washington newspaper stories are
about an event that happened yesterday, today, or is expected to happen
tomorrow; the figure for network television is 10 percent higher. (The
contention that television news is a headline service is borne out to this
extent.)

The concentration on events also allows an efficient use of staff. A reporter
sent to cover a trial, a major congressional hearing, or a cabinet officer's
briefing, almost always comes back with a story. The average time spent on
stories that do not pan out is only about three hours a week.[17] On the other
hand, in so-called enterprise reporting, which is not tied to a daily event,
journalists often complain of "digging dry holes." In an extreme case, an
editor notes that one of his reporters spent six months examining records of
a prominent official's land deals with "no payoff; the story was not used."

Whether an event is covered or not is influenced to some small degree by
the medium: newspapers give more attention than television to reports and
studies; television devotes more attention to public meetings.[18] The latter
provides more visual opportunities than the former. Yet the difference should
not be overstated. Despite the assumption that rallies and demonstrations are
staged because of the notice they will receive from the cameras, television
does not focus significantly more on this category. Television and newspapers
share the same definition of news; they cover the same events regardless of
technical differences. Even when a location is off-limits to cameras, the
networks run a story if the event rates high enough among the day's other
events. Although there is a ban on filming in Washington courtrooms,
television and newspapers have just about the same percentage of stories on
judicial events. Television technologists, in these cases, revert to that most
ancient form of communication, the drawing.

Eighty percent of Washington stories are about events. Wire service and
radio reporters most often write hard news. Beats notable for producing a
high percentage of hard news are the Supreme Court, diplomacy, and

17. The number of hours depends on experience: reporters in their twenties average four
and a half hours a week, which drops to nearly two hours for those in their thirties.

18. Thirteen percent of Washington stories in newspapers and 6 percent of those on network
television news include information about the release of reports or studies. Public meetings are
reported in 15 percent of Washington stories on network television and in 7 percent of
Washington stories in newspapers.

Congress. A quarter of the Washington press corps express concern over the media's heavy accent on hard news (breaking news); another 25 percent say this is a problem, but not "serious"; half do not put this in a problem category. Those who work for the organizations that specialize in hard news and those whose beats (except for diplomacy) deal in events are most likely to think that the press gives too much attention to these events.

Are reporters once again merely exercising their constitutional right to complain? Dissatisfaction with the emphasis on hard news/breaking news is fashionable in the press corps. There are those who talk of longing to write in-depth stories if only their editors were more enlightened. But clues suggest that if reporters were entirely free agents they would cover the same news in much the same manner. Class A general assignment reporters—the group with the most leeway to choose their own stories—produce exactly the same ratio of hard news to soft news as other reporters (eighty to twenty). And older reporters, who have more clout in their organizations, use it to get better assignments, not to write a different type of story. The four to one ratio actually seems to be a happy balance between the excitement of chasing fires (or the Washington equivalent) and pleasure of reflective writing, between the gratification of being on the front page and the gratification of publishing long, contemplative pieces. The ratio of hard news to soft news also corresponds to newspapers' needs for weekday news and Sunday features.

The primary mission of the mass media is as a daily chronicle, a not unimportant reason why news workers choose journalism in the first place. "The nature of the business has always been breaking news," notes a regional reporter for a newspaper chain, "and if you can't handle it, you shouldn't be here."

At the same time, nearly 8 percent of newspaper stories are interpretive.[19] As breaking news is more and more reported first on television, newspapers are shifting emphasis slightly from *what* to *why*. Some organizations prohibit their reporters from doing opinion pieces ("If they call Kissinger dumb in a column, will Kissinger be willing to grant them an interview later?" asks one editor), but others find that interpretive articles allow reporters to give vent to creative impulses, producing better staff morale; that they are good pieces for the enlarged op-ed pages and Sunday commentary sections; and that they cut down on reporters' free-lance activities (sometimes done on the employers' time). Charles Peters, editor and founder of the *Washington Monthly*, recounts that when he began publishing in 1969 he had considerable success

19. Stories on politics, economics/finance, and defense rate well above average in interpretive writing; stories about law, regulatory policy, and energy are lower than average.

attracting reporters as contributors, because the opportunity was not often available in their own newspapers. But "there has been a great opening up of opinion and analysis pieces in papers," he says, "and I have almost stopped propositioning these guys."

THE WAY news is gathered turns clichés about experience paying off and contacts being very important into prophecies. A story is a mosaic of facts and quotations from sources who are participants in an event or who have knowledge about it. To get the story a reporter must know whom to ask, who will answer the phone, who is apt to talk.

The research tool is the interview. Washington journalists conducted 3,967 interviews for 865 stories—or close to five interviews per story.[20] News gathering, then, often boils down to the skill of the individual reporter at getting his or her sources to say things that are newsworthy. Interview journalism is not unique to Washington, but distance from the home office enhances the value of contacts, which strengthen reporters' autonomy and protect them from competition.

News is skewed by those who are most willing to talk. It takes two for an interview. Oral research, by definition, requires access. "On Capitol Hill you always have access," says an experienced newsman. "Congressmen figure you win some and you lose some. It's different with an administration. [President] Kennedy canceled his subscription to the *New York Herald Tribune* because he didn't like something it published. Who ever heard of a congressman canceling his newspaper subscription?" Reliance on oral research makes a reporter risk becoming "the prisoner of the source,"[21] particularly of sources in the executive branch, where information can be more tightly controlled than on Capitol Hill. (The possibilities of finding multiple sources in Congress make it a preferred location for news gathering.)

The interview technique is not equally advantageous. Television interviews have logistics/equipment problems, and the camera sometimes has an inhibiting effect. Newsmakers have less incentive to talk to reporters for noninfluential outlets. Old-timers are advantaged over newcomers. (A veteran reporter for a small newspaper claims that the disadvantage of his place of employment is more than compensated for by the advantage of his seniority

20. These figures relate to each reporter's longest story of the day. But reporters also do short pieces, often based on press releases rather than interviews, such as the awarding of a grant to a local community or an appointment to an advisory council.

21. See John Rothchild, "Views of the Press: The Stories Reporters Don't Write," *Washington Monthly*, vol. 3 (June 1971), pp. 20–27.

in the press corps.) Reporters for the print media are advantaged in their dealings with their home offices, since interviews are a form of private communication, not readily subject to verification.

Washington reporters use no documents in the preparation of nearly three-quarters of their stories. (Press releases are not counted as documents.) The research file of most reporters is a desk drawer of press clippings. When reporters do use documents, they rely most often (nearly a third of the time) on newspaper articles, "verifying" information by referring to what they or their colleagues wrote before. Given that most copy is produced under deadline conditions and other hardships, research that rests heavily on other newspaper stories bears a high potential for perpetuating error.

Few Washington news operations have their own facilities for serious documents research. The typical bureau owns a small collection of standard reference books and subscribes to general circulation magazines. Some bureau chiefs argue that a sizable library is not necessary because it would duplicate that in the home office. Reporters, however, claim that they rarely make use of headquarters facilities, citing the time factor. But even when good facilities are at hand, there is not much evidence that reporters rely on them. A Washington bureau librarian says, "Reporters' inquiries are very simple, spelling of names, middle initials, piddling things. I have not had a request for in-depth research for quite some time." Perhaps this is because the government provides so much "public information"; Washington reporters contact press secretaries or public information offices on almost half of their stories.

A reporter complains, "[My organization] wastes time and money by having us do research that someone who would earn half of what we do could do." But few reporters—only a third, mostly on newspapers—show any enthusiasm for more researchers or research facilities when prompted by interviewers' questions. They seem to take pride in not using researchers. Says a magazine writer, "I skin my own skunks." Asked about the absence of researchers at a large newspaper bureau, the chief responds, "Reporters should do their own research." This is the way it always has been done.

Reliance on interviews and documents differs depending on assignment. On the politics and diplomacy beats, reporters get the vast majority of their information through interviewing. Those on the economics and Supreme Court beats rely more heavily on documents. Science reporters are above the average in the use of both documents and interviews. White House reporters use the fewest documents. The beats with a high-interview/low-documents profile are usually rated the most desirable and also rank high on the events-coverage scale. While reporters agree that regulatory agencies are not sufficiently covered, they do not want the assignment: heavy reliance on documents makes the beat "dull," "boring," "drudgery"—words that are repeated over and over.[22]

Poring over documents may be too time-consuming to be a useful tool in covering breaking news. Yet when newspaper and television reporters are given more time to do stories, they simply do more interviews. A reason for their shunning of documents research may be a lack of training. A small newspaper publisher claims that of hundreds of applicants for reporting jobs he cannot recall one with course work in accounting, a skill he feels is particularly valuable in news gathering. (His comment suggests a limit of journalism when practiced almost exclusively through oral research.)

In a press corps that must interview to survive, systems develop to increase access. Reporters organize themselves for the purpose of holding regular meetings with news sources. One group, primarily newspaper bureau chiefs, was started in 1966 and had nearly 800 private breakfast sessions with newsmakers by mid-1977. Another group is made up mostly of the "number two" people in the bureaus. There is a group restricted to young reporters. Other groups are arranged by specialization, such as environment and energy. Groups tend to be composed of prime competitors, so rivals get the same information and others are excluded. One participant in a prestigious group, run by Godfrey Sperling of the *Christian Science Monitor*, says that its importance to him is in getting "a feel for what other reporters are interested in based on their questioning."

The chief way reporters increase access is by offering news sources a degree of anonymity, ranging from "off the record" (reporters cannot use the information) to "deep background" (reporters can use the information only on their own authority) to "background" (reporters can use the information but cannot name the source, although they can ascribe the source, as in "An administration official said. . . ."). Such rituals, if not unique to Washington, are far more prevalent there than in the rest of the country. "It took me a long time to learn that game," says a newspaper reporter. "In Binghamton, you were either on the record or I didn't listen."

Reporters indicate that 28 percent of their interviews are off the record or background. Content analysis shows that 13 percent of the quotations in

22. Over half the reporters consider lack of regulatory agencies coverage a serious problem; most of these work for newspapers, magazines, and television networks. Less than 16 percent of the reporters say it is not a problem.

newspaper stories are not attributed to a name and do not give readers enough information to determine whether the source has a special interest; the figure for the television network evening news programs drops to 8 percent, sources who will not appear on camera being less valuable to a visual medium.[23]

Nonattribution rises as stories gain in importance or if they deal with national security.[24] "In foreign affairs, news is more delicate since you're dealing with other countries," says a diplomatic reporter for a leading newspaper. Yet this does not fully explain the Washington reporter's penchant for not naming sources. Stories in twenty-five subject categories, regardless of their sensitivity, contain unidentified quotations: 11 percent of the stories about housing and urban affairs, 10 percent of the agriculture stories, and 6 percent of the stories on education. Reporters suggest reasons: "[Secretary of State] Vance on a plane will give absolutely useless information, but by putting it on background it will seem more important or revealing and so it will get into print." "It would hurt the copy to identify the number three person in the NSC [National Security Council]." "Sometimes I wonder whether I could have gotten an unnamed source to go on record if I had just tried harder."

Critics fault the practice of nonattribution because it fails to hold officials accountable; reporters respond that the information would not be otherwise available. Only because "background statements have deniability" (says a wire service reporter) will officials talk at all. Seventy-one percent of the reporters think that the public gains from not-for-attribution practices; 17 percent think the public loses. In their relations with their employers, the reporters always gain—the conventions of background journalism, Washington-style, are one more way reporters increase their autonomy.[25]

23. Stories are considered attributed even if a name is not given if there is other relevant information about who was making a statement. For example, a story about a day in the life of a Secret Service agent is an attributable story, although the agent's name is never mentioned. It is clear from comparing versions of a reporter's story in different newspapers that editors are often responsible for deleting the names of sources.

24. Not-for-attribution information is contained in 8 percent more of the stories that appear on the front page than in the stories that do not make page 1. "Blind" quotations appear five times as often in stories about foreign policy and defense than in stories about transportation and health.

25. Even in the Watergate exposé, when the reputation of the *Washington Post* rested on the accuracy of information presented through two relatively inexperienced reporters, Woodward and Bernstein say that they never revealed the name of the source they called Deep Throat to publisher Katherine Graham and editor Ben Bradlee. See Carl Bernstein and Bob Woodward, *All the President's Men* (Simon and Schuster, 1974), pp. 146, 236.

WASHINGTON reporters need not suffer from job insecurity; few reporters get fired. Still, they live in a world of competition and uncertainty. Events seem to happen faster now, actions are more complex. As their stories become more important, so too do the stakes. The reporter is alone, except for other reporters—friends, but also rivals. The reporter's work is exposed: there it is on the front page or the network evening news. Yet it can never be the whole story, and it may be proved wrong tomorrow. Moreover, reporters think of themselves as serious people, and they take their work seriously.

Of course, reporters do not confront a series of moral dilemmas every time they sit down at their typewriters: many stories are quite straightforward; some reporters are not capable of seeing the complexity of the world they cover or the work they do; and other reporters may subconsciously simplify events as a way of limiting uncertainty and controlling their environment. It is not necessary to picture every Washington journalist as a brooding Hamlet to make the case that their world is a dangerous place. Their complaining, though often misdirected, has a basis.

A paradox of journalism is that the work of journalists remains highly competitive at a time when the news business is becoming less competitive. Fewer and fewer cities have more than one newspaper or different owners for morning and afternoon papers. There are two domestic wire services (there used to be three) and three commercial television networks (there used to be four). But competition between reporters is not economic. This attitude depresses salaries while increasing time and money spent on a story. Competition is "more professional than real," says a veteran writer for a newsmagazine, who means that the primary object of his labors is not to sell more magazines.

In a sense, every Washington reporter is in competition with every other reporter. Nor is the competition merely for exclusive stories. A newsmagazine reporter, part of a two-person team at the White House, speaks of tensions when competing "against the person you're working with." Newspaper reporters compete for space with those in their own organization, with wire service reporters, and with reporters whose copy is transmitted through a supplemental news service. Many editors have four versions of the same story to choose from. There is competition between reporters on the same beat, even when they have no readers or listeners in common; reporters from morning and afternoon papers in the same city are in competition, even though their papers have the same ownership and modest overlapping circulations; the *Washington Post* and the *New York Times* compete, although they are in different cities.[26] Newswork attracts highly competitive people,[27] and if no direct competition exists, reporters invent it.

Yet to describe the Washington press corps exclusively in terms of competition is to picture a human jungle that does not exist. Reporters also cooperate with each other, and cooperation gives way to competition only as information becomes valuable.[28] Cooperation is a product of friendship, fraternity, and self-protection. Journalism has a tradition of fraternal sharing, of exchanging information of routine nature, and of older reporters helping newcomers. An old-timer tells of a day with President Harry Truman at Key West when one of the regular reporters was too drunk to file a story. Independently, three of his colleagues sent their "blacks" (the carbons of their own stories) to the inebriated friend's editor. "I liked the second version of your story best," wired the editor.

In a business that does not rely on documents research, "other reporters are our information bank," says a reporter for a major newspaper. "When I was doing a story on Mondale, I went to reporters who had covered him in Minnesota." The historical memory of the press corps, however, is limited by the modest number of elders in its ranks.

Cooperation that grows out of friendships and fraternity exists wherever there are journalists; cooperation for self-protection, based on the need to limit uncertainty, is most often evident where reporters work at a distance from the home office. Here one finds an "us against them" attitude, Washington reporters versus home offices. Self-protective cooperation is found most among reporters on beats that cover major events, where editors are likely to notice differences between rival stories. These are the beats given to older reporters, who are most apt to have known each other for years, and the beats on which reporters work in the closest proximity, in a pressroom or on a press bus. These reporters are also more likely than those on other beats to switch employers, so that over time a competitor may become a colleague.

26. Chalmers M. Roberts writes, "The way the *Post* knew what the *Times* was printing that evening was that each night it received from New York via UPI wirephoto a picture of page 1 of the *Times'* first edition, on the street early enough for the *Post* to catch up in its main edition. The *Times* received a similar facsimile from Washington." See *The Washington Post: The First 100 Years* (Houghton Mifflin, 1977), p. 393.

27. When studying the home office of the *New York Times*, Chris Argyris found that "100 percent of the news people described their colleagues as very competitive." See *Behind the Front Page* (Jossey-Bass, 1974), p. 10.

28. "Readily available information is shared; privately developed information rarely is," writes Gaye Tuchman in *Making News: A Study in the Construction of Reality* (Free Press, 1978), p. 75.

A newcomer to the political press corps tells of hearing a reporter for an influential newspaper calling in his story in a voice much louder than necessary. Was he cuing his friends about the lead he had chosen? The young man notes with bitterness that such survival techniques lend a hand to lazy colleagues, carrying along the least conscientious. It is also a way that reporters minimize the threat of an uneasy environment and the control of their bosses.

CHAPTER TWO

ꟷews Organizations

IN THE SOLAR system of Washington news gathering, the sun—source of light, heat, and energy—is the political government (notably the president and Congress), and Washington news organizations are its planets. They form three rings, an inner ring, a ring of middle distance, and an outermost ring.

In Washington, reporters say, "access is the name of the game," and closeness to the center usually determines access: for example, newsmakers regularly leak information to those who work for the organizations of the inner ring, less often to others. When the New York Times was on strike in 1978, the bureau chief of a middle-ring operation noted, "The leak group expanded, and we started getting some goodies too."

The system is inequitable, of course. But there are correctives by which individual reporters who work for middle-ring organizations can gain entry to the inner ring—as individuals. Few other occupations have invented so many prizes and awards to honor its workers. These are often won by reporters of middle-ring organizations, who, except for bad luck or other reasons not related to ability, would work for inner-ring operations. Almost nothing, however, will elevate reporters of the outer ring to the inner ring.

The inner ring consists of the three television networks, the two wire services, the three weekly newsmagazines, and four newspapers.[1] The national media—television networks, newsmagazines, and wire services—are important to the political government, because through them it learns what the country is learning about what it is doing.[2] (The wire services provide the majority of Washington stories to most newspapers and radio stations and in

---

1. These are the American Broadcasting Company, the Columbia Broadcasting System, the National Broadcasting Company; the Associated Press, the United Press International; Newsweek, Time, U.S. News & World Report; the Washington Post, the New York Times, the Washington Star, and the Wall Street Journal.

2. Washington reporters claim they watch an average of one network weekday evening news program a day, and three-quarters say they read at least one newsmagazine each week; two-thirds rate the wire services as important in their work.

a sense are surrogates for the outer ring.) But the political government and the press keep in touch with each other primarily through the four newspapers.

"Everyone needs a reference point," says a newsmagazine bureau chief. The newspapers of the inner ring are the reference point of Washington journalism. A point of reference is not a definition of news and is only marginally connected to the selection of stories. Rather, the papers of the inner ring set the tone. For the mass of reporters, looking over their shoulders at these papers, this means being very serious. Not all reporters aspire to work in the inner ring, but one suspects most would like to think of themselves "in the tradition of," much as schools of artists are labeled.

Newspaper read regularly	Reporters (percent)[3]	High federal officials (percent)[4]
Washington Post	89	90
New York Times	73	45
Washington Star	59	n.a.
Wall Street Journal	51	62
Los Angeles Times	5	4

The drop from the inner ring to the middle ring—from fourth to fifth "most read" newspaper in political Washington—is precipitous. And neither the size nor the quality of its Washington bureau assures a newspaper membership in the inner ring. The *Los Angeles Times* began in the mid-1960s to assemble a large and talented Washington staff, many hired away from a financially faltering inner-ring organization, the *New York Herald Tribune*. These reporters brought their standing with them, including memberships in journalism's more exclusive social clubs, professional associations, and background groups. Yet a vastly improved newspaper raised the

3. Reporters were asked which newspapers they read daily. Their reading of their own newspapers or rival newspapers in the same city is not included.

A former *Washington Post* reporter warns, "Don't exaggerate how much newsmen read. What always stunned me as a newsman is how few non-page-1 *Post* stories outside their immediate 'beat' or professional concerns my colleagues had read or even scanned." Even with this caveat, the rankings—which reflect responses to open-ended questions—suggest the order in which reporters believe various news outlets are important, that is, what they think they should read.

4. Data from Wall Street Journal, Marketing Services Department, *Opinion Leaders*, vol. 1 (Dow Jones, 1979), p. 17. Officials were asked which newspapers they read regularly, meaning "an average of at least three of every four issues." The *Washington Star* is not included in the survey (n.a. meaning not available).

paper only to the top of the middle ring. The leaders of government, commerce, labor, and the news media do not live in Los Angeles.

In the middle ring are, at the moment, seven independent newspapers and two newspaper chains.[5]

Newspaper read at least once a week	Reporters (percent)[6]
Los Angeles Times	21
Baltimore Sun	16
Boston Globe	13
Christian Science Monitor	9
Chicago Tribune	7
Knight-Ridder newspapers	7
Journal of Commerce (New York)	6
New York Daily News	4
Cox newspapers	4

This group has no natural boundaries; its membership ebbs and flows, unlike the inner ring, which is likely to change only if an operation goes out of business.

As telling as who is "in" is who is "out." Numbers do not insure status: the Thomson organization has seventy U.S. newspapers. Circulation does not insure status: the Hearst organization owns papers in Los Angeles, San Francisco, Seattle, Baltimore, Boston, Albany, and San Antonio.[7] To gain entrance to the middle ring, an enterprise must be of serious intent, willing to commit a substantial amount of money to its Washington office, and the money must be spent in prescribed ways.

The standing of a news organization that orbits the political government is thus determined by four criteria. *Scope,* or national orientation: the more local a news organization's interests, the lower its position. It loses points for being "provincial." *Resources,* or number of reporters and the amount they

5. Knight-Ridder papers listed were the *Philadelphia Inquirer,* the *Miami Herald,* and the *Detroit Free Press;* Cox papers listed were the *Atlanta Constitution* and the *Atlanta Journal.* (Four magazines of opinion—the *New Yorker,* the *New Republic,* the *Atlantic,* and *Harper's,* in that order—have sufficient readership among reporters to qualify for the middle ring. But except for the *New Republic,* which has its headquarters in Washington, they cannot be said to have much visible *organizational* presence in Washington. Rather, some of their writers, such as Elizabeth Drew of the *New Yorker* and John Osborne of the *New Republic* have inner-ring standing as individuals.)

6. Reporters reading their own newspapers or rival papers in the same city are not included.

7. Since outreach is a minimal requirement for status, it might be said that the Gannett organization, most of whose newspapers have circulations under 50,000, acquired the "chance" to move up to the middle ring by buying papers in Wilmington, Nashville, Cincinnati, and Oakland. The Thomson organization also continues to add U.S. newspapers, but they are all in small communities.

travel: a news organization must maintain at least six full-time national reporters in Washington and must locate them in certain places—including the White House and the State Department. It loses points for using wire service copy for its main stories. *Audience*, or the characteristics of readers or listeners: is the audience important, either in numbers or as elites? The *New York Times*, the *Los Angeles Times*, and the *Washington Post* vastly expanded their audiences by selling their reportage to other papers. The *Baltimore Sun* counts elites in its readership, since it is available in Washington on day of publication. *Purpose*, seriousness of function: is the parent operation perceived by the press corps as primarily in the business of making money, entertaining, or educating? Being educational is mandatory to gain high standing; only then is it acceptable to be profitable and entertaining.

On these criteria the *Baltimore Sun*, for example, is high in the middle ring. Its bureau has twelve reporters, twice the minimum requirement for middle-ring eligibility. Its coverage is heavily national (only one reporter is assigned to regional news), and it rarely runs a Washington wire service story on page 1. It is read by Washington journalists and high government officials since Baltimore is just forty miles from the capital. Middle-ring papers from some cities—Los Angeles, Atlanta, Boston—have to go to considerable expense to get day-of-publication delivery to those they consider very important readers in Washington. But the *Sun's* weekday circulation is only 180,000 (giving it the highest ratio of Washington reporters to readers of any major news organization), and it does not sell its copy to other news organizations as most other middle-ring operations do.

The *Sun* hires reporters from the low inner ring and loses reporters to the high inner ring: a *Washington Star* reporter may go to the *Sun*, a *Sun* reporter may go to the *New York Times* or the *Washington Post*. Although stepping down in organizational status to step up in assignment is rare (most upgrading in assignment is done through a lateral change in organization), middle-ring operations such as the *Sun* attract and hold top reporters by offering opportunities to do analysis and interpretation, not an automatic characteristic of inner-ring jobs.

Individuals in Washington operations of fewer than six reporters may become middle-ringers through specialization, investigative reporting, or outside activities, such as writing books (including novels) and appearing on television.[8] But the typical reporter in the outer ring must rely heavily on

---

8. At one time, all three reporters in the Washington bureau of the *Des Moines Register* had won Pulitzer Prizes for investigative journalism.

official access—press conferences, press releases, and public information offices. It is not just that their employers lack clout; they are also spread too thin to have close encounters in high places.

Reporters working exclusively for radio are automatically in the outer ring. Radio is national in reach, but its standard five-minute format—with three minutes of news—is too abbreviated to be taken seriously by Washington reporters. "At [my organization] there is not journalism," says a radio network newscaster, "just little news items cleverly organized around commercial time." Too, radio relies extensively on the wire services, lacking reporters at the places where news is being made.

Specialized publications, independent television stations, regional news services, and small newspapers are sometimes in the outer ring, but only if they seek their energy from the political government. More often, these organizations are in other solar systems. Most specialized publications, for example, orbit around the permanent government;[9] regional news services, television stations, and small papers focus on a few legislators (a city or state congressional delegation). In their own solar systems, they are the inner ring. When they move into the presidential or congressional system they become part of the outer ring.

WASHINGTON news gathering is actually several worlds—a world of specialized publications, a world of regional news services, a world of radio, and so forth:

Organization	Reporters (percent)[10]
Television network	6
Radio station	6
Television station	1
Broadcast total	13
Independent newspaper	27
Chain newspaper	11
Specialized publication	25
Wire service	11
Magazine	10
Regional news service	4
Print total	88

9. Two specialized publications (both weeklies)—the *Congressional Quarterly* and the *National Journal*—are in the political solar system; their reporters can be thought of as in the middle ring. Specialized publications that are not in the political solar system have a different personnel profile.

10. Percentages are rounded, so total does not equal 100.

There is very little interaction between these worlds. (Interactions come on the beat, which is the subject of the next chapter.) Washington reporters know little about organizations unlike their own. They live in their own worlds out of preference even though this severely limits employment possibilities. When they change jobs they tend to stay in the same type of organization. Of all job moves, 36 percent are from newspaper to newspaper, 14 percent from radio to radio, 10 percent from specialized publication to specialized publication. Only 9 percent move from print to broadcast or from broadcast to print, most of them prominent newspaper reporters switching to the networks. (The horizons are always wider at the top of a trade, and the usual rules of advancement do not apply. Thus, for example, Carl Bernstein, the *Washington Post* reporter of Watergate fame, became the bureau chief of ABC-TV.)

Many companies are horizontal conglomerates, owning newspapers, television stations, radio stations, and magazines. Yet they maintain Washington bureaus for each type of operation. One group of reporters works for Cox Newspapers and another group for Cox Broadcasting; even the wire services have different staffs for print and radio. Some companies have separate bureaus for their small and large newspapers.[11] Some of these separations are historical, but most reflect functional differences.

WHILE there is no longer the tension between newspaper and television news gathering that characterized the early days of television—partly because television equipment is now less intrusive—there remains on the part of television people a defensiveness rarely heard from newspaper people. Those in television complain that others restrict the use of their equipment, that the equipment is inflexible, that the networks devote inadequate time and money to news. They speak of the constant search for pictures to illustrate their stories. Often the complaints are comparisons with print journalism:

They can ask fifteen questions before we set up the lights. . . . We have
an earlier break-off point than print because we need more time to
produce a story for broadcast. . . . We can get sound and picture from
the moon, but not from the Senate. . . . If visuals are weak, the story
may not be played as well. . . . My network gets tired of me standing
in front of the row of limp flags at the State Department. . . . They can
publish stories that are not of immediate concern, stories that can run

11. For example, Dow Jones maintains different Washington bureaus for the *Wall Street Journal* and the Ottaway newspapers; the parent company of the *New York Times* has a separate bureau for the chain of Florida newspapers that it owns.

on page 56. On TV only the major stories run, which make officials more willing to talk with print reporters. . . . You can't have a meeting in a dark garage with Deep Throat if you have two cameras and four people. . . . [My network] with its $400 million cash reserves should have as many reporters in Washington as the Washington Post.

The belief that television is a less serious news form is most pronounced among older television network correspondents, who then write books and articles to remind themselves and their colleagues that they are still journalists of standing. There is more involved than self-image—television reporters do read more newspapers than newspaper reporters watch television.[12] Still, these figures are also related to age: older reporters in both media read more newspapers *and* watch more televised news than younger reporters. They are the news freaks, as a veteran magazine bureau chief calls himself. And in Washington television, despite television's reputation for accenting youth—the so-called pretty face syndrome—nearly one-fifth of the network reporters are over fifty years old. "TV reporters have miserable lives," says a television reporter. "They travel all the time. That's why a lot of senior people come to Washington—to settle down." Senior people also have no place else to go unless they choose to quit television or to anchor a local news program.[13] While print reporters may become editors or even publishers, television reporters rarely get to be executives. There are separate career tracks—on-camera and off-camera—and the choice is made initially.

But the first generation of television news reporters, who came from newspapers and wire services (though often by way of radio), is now approaching retirement. Those at the tail end of this generation are crossing their fiftieth-year mark. The second generation, coming from local stations, was hired by the networks after evening news programs were expanded from fifteen minutes to half an hour in 1963. No "farm system" has developed for producing future network reporters or to pave the route to Washington, mecca for network correspondents.[14] Who gets picked to move from local

12. Television reporters also claim they read more newspapers than do newspaper reporters. For example, 95 percent of TV reporters—but only 55 percent of newspaper reporters—claim they read both the *New York Times* and the *Washington Post* daily.

13. Another alternative is public television. Examples, over the years, include former network correspondents Martin Agronsky, Paul Duke, Robert MacNeil, Bill Moyers, and Sander Vanocur. There has been a more modest reverse flow, reporters moving from public radio and television to the commercial outlets. However, the percentage of reporters making such moves is statistically insignificant. Also, in 1980, the first major cable television news bureau was opened in Washington, with Daniel Schorr, formerly of CBS, as its chief correspondent.

14. In the week of 1978, 45 percent of reporters seen on camera were based in Washington. A 1973 study reports that 40 percent of the television network evening news stories originate in

station to network location other than Washington and then to the Washington bureau is still idiosyncratic, often influenced by which local reporters are noticed when their stories are picked up by national news programs.

According to conventional wisdom (formulated by newspaper people), news on the television networks is heavily influenced by the newspapers of the inner ring, particularly the *Times* since the networks have their head-quarters in New York. However, the top events of the day, the staple of television news, appear on the evening programs the day before they are published in the *Times*. A television executive, who makes a lot of the Washington assignments, comments, "Where do they influence us? First, if they are into a major investigative story, given our limited investigative resources. Second, if they are treating an issue as being very, very serious over time, especially if it's an issue we're treating summarily. Third, there's a process of osmosis in their editorials, op-ed columns, and news emphasis that filters down, but it's hard to define. And fourth, they're a check on us. If they play a story a different way, we'll look twice the next time."

Because the gap between newspaper reading and television news viewing is narrower among younger reporters, and for other reasons, perhaps the next generation of television workers will not use newspapers as their reference point. (The models for one younger celebrity of network news when growing up in a small midwestern town were Chet Huntley and David Brinkley; but who were their models?) Perhaps too, like the younger generation of filmmakers, the newer television news gatherers will become enamored of the nonlinear way of telling a story. Today the reporter who says, "I like the creative possibilities of combining words and videotape—the techniques and mechanics of it fascinate me," is a rarity. With such changes the demarcation between print and television will become more pronounced, and reporters' skills less transferable.

Television requires a much more structured news operation than news-papers. It is the creature of a high technology that demands planning. It is part of a larger enterprise. More people are involved in producing a story. Each story must conform to rigid time specifications, since the time of a television program is inelastic (except in unusual circumstances, as when a president dies).

Newspaper space is elastic; it can be expanded or cut to fit the news (or advertising). And because of the genius of newspaper writing style—an

---

the capital. See Michael J. Robinson, "American Political Legitimacy in an Era of Electronic Journalism: Reflections on the Evening News," in Douglass Cater and Richard Adler, eds., *Television as a Social Force: New Approaches to TV Criticism* (Praeger, 1975), p. 116.

inverted pyramid, which rank orders facts according to their importance—each story can be cut from the bottom up. Television newswriting, on the other hand, perhaps because it developed in an entertainment medium, is shaped to follow fictive form, with beginning, middle, and end.[15] Once the story is produced, it usually is used or not used as a unit.

Even at the news gathering level, television is a collaborative undertaking. "Newspaper reporters need a notebook, pencil, and a telephone. We're a traveling production unit," says a television network correspondent, a former newspaper reporter. Filming, sound, lighting, words, editing involve a degree of coordination, cooperation, negotiation—and control—that is unnecessary at comparable stages on newspapers. Newspaper people see themselves as following in a tradition of individualism, even when they are acting otherwise; television newspeople, as their journalistic descendants, would like to maintain this tradition, but it is a luxury that the technology and structuring of their medium cannot indulge. They must have co-workers.

In addition to working for the network evening news programs (and radio), television correspondents do stories for the early morning programs. In many cases the A.M. reports are the ones that did not make last night's programs. Still, they involve extra labor as a new beginning ("top") has to be written. Some reporters also appear on the Sunday interview programs and make documentaries.

All evidence indicates that beat for beat—though obviously not reporter for reporter—television news gatherers work longer hours than their print counterparts. With justifiable exaggeration, a television correspondent at the White House says, "When print reporters are through, we are just beginning to work. Most of our time is spent on the logistics of trying to get on the air." However, the work load in the network bureaus is not equally divided. Those at the top work hardest. This is not the rule in newspaper bureaus, where young reporters produce more stories (although they are relatively short and less likely to be on the front page), and on newsmagazines, where older reporters often have the less strenuous assignments. But in television the reporters on the major beats produce the most stories and also put in the most time on each story. A State Department correspondent explains, "Those on general assignment are sent out as an extension of the camera and don't have to do a lot of background interviewing."

RADIO reporters usually find jobs in Washington after three or four years on local stations, but they do not then move to television. The comments of a

    15. See Paul H. Weaver, "Is Television News Biased?" *Public Interest*, no. 26 (Winter 1972), p. 67.

majority of radio reporters suggest that they think of themselves as having the worst of all worlds, the various disadvantages of electronic journalism—equipment that jams, recorders that run out of tape, newsmakers who are "reluctant to speak frankly with a microphone in their face"—without the advantages of prestige and high pay that come to many of their counterparts in television and newspapers:

> Radio is the most perishable of all mediums so editors are more indifferent to what you do. . . . I do not now consider myself a journalist, but rather a wire service rewrite man who blabs on the radio. . . . [My operation] is a garbage can that they are constantly having to fill by scrounging around for stories. . . . The [radio] newscaster typically has little direct contact with newsmakers or news events. . . . The only thing they [television networks] leave for radio are the crumbs from the table. Radio is thought to be the least legitimate, it is the bottom of the pecking order.

The only radio reporters who are very pleased with their jobs are several of the youngest (happy to be in journalism at all) and blacks covering news of special interest to blacks, who see their work as providing a much needed service.

At the same time, many network television correspondents find doing stories for radio satisfying. A diplomatic correspondent likes radio work when he is traveling abroad, seeing it almost as a catharsis—a way to report news that there would not be room for on television. A Supreme Court reporter uses radio as a warm-up: "The more often I write a story for radio, the more polished it is for the TV evening news." Enthusiasts for radio feel it is a purer news form, permitting the reporter to concentrate on content. "When I'm on TV I think about other things than the story—like 'look at the camera'." "On TV stories I have to be aware of the pieces of film and their length. Radio allows me to work out what the story is all about without having to keep these factors in mind."

ALMOST one of four Washington reporters works for the specialized press, clearly a growth industry. These publications spring to life in response to new government activities or programs whose constituencies need facts not available in the daily newspaper (like *Sludge*, which biweekly informs its 35,000 readers about air pollution control residues, hazardous industrial-process waste, and related subjects). Typically, they are competent compilations of federal regulations, court decisions, personnel announcements, notices of contracts being let, new grant application procedures, and other types of government data, long on facts and short on style and interpretation.

Limited journalism experience need not be a serious handicap. And, indeed, these are the only major Washington news organizations with substantial numbers of young reporters.

There are some giants in the field—the Bureau of National Affairs publishes over fifty newsletters and similar publications—but most are small operations. Very few mass media reporters have any clear sense of their presence. Specialized publications cannot be purchased at newsstands; they usually have very high subscription rates; and their reporters are most often found inside bureaucracies or at obscure congressional hearings.

Specialized publications form their own solar system, revolving around the permanent government. The workers give their organizations the highest rating for "informing the public" and rate themselves high in job satisfaction (although not "very" satisfied). Salaries are low, and few reporters stay on beyond their thirties.

ONLY a decade ago the capital landscape was dotted with regional news services selling local-angle stories, usually about the activities of a community's congressional representative. *Regional* (as distinct from *national*) describes both the news covered and the clients, who were clustered in a state or section of the country. One operation concentrated on Oregon, another on Michigan, and so on, and typically worked for a half-dozen independent papers, each too small to afford to maintain its own Washington bureau. Today a regional operation may represent only two or three papers. In 1968, for example, the Sarah McClendon Bureau covered Washington for four Texas dailies—three of them are now owned by chains with their own bureaus. (McClendon now spends most of her time writing a column that is distributed through a small West Coast syndicate.)

Reporters at regional services are either young or old by Washington press standards. The young do not plan to stay there very long; the old-timers are the entrepreneurs who own the operations, a crusty lot bearing the scars of trying to maintain their independence at the fringes of national journalism.[16] They think that the regional news service reporter plays a uniquely useful role, "but I wouldn't want my daughter to marry one." They see themselves "becoming a scarce breed," says another, "I have had more horses shot out from under me by economic conditions beyond my control than General Custer did. . . . I think in the end we face financial extinction."

16. Reporters in their twenties working for the regional news services have a different profile from reporters covering regional news for independent and chain papers. The news service reporters have considerably more education, attended more selective schools, and are likely to talk about wanting to work for the elite news outlets.

THE TWO giant American wire services—Associated Press and United Press International—form the bone structure of Washington news gathering. Their reporters keep track of the basic events, constantly updating developments. Explains a sixty-two-year-old wire service reporter, "I normally do a story three or more times—in late afternoon or evening for P.M. papers of the following day, a lead by noon, again for A.M. papers, and sometimes another lead. Then the cycle starts over again." Each day at noon the wires also alert their clients to the top stories, providing a type of nationwide agenda.

Wire service employment is an anomaly in the pecking order of newswork: low-prestige jobs in inner-ring organizations. Washington reporters rate the product high but, at the same time, only a third of them claim they would work for the wires—compared, for example, with four of five who say they would like to be employed by magazines.[17] Even jobs in radio rank higher. One reason is probably creativity: although the wire services are beginning to encourage investigative reporting and interpretive writing, their reputation is founded on nuts-and-bolts reportage. Another problem is anonymity: wire service stories often appear without a by-line. Editors are not motivated to give credit to reporters not on their staffs. Nor are the wires high-paying operations, at least by the scale of other inner-ring organizations. And some reporters may shy away from what might seem to be an exceptionally wearing life.

Certainly the wire service people produce more words per day than the average reporter, but they do not work more hours per week. They are far from being burnt-out cases. Among Washington reporters, wire service reporters rate their job satisfaction the highest, are least likely to say that there is "some work other than journalism that [they] would like to do someday," and stay in reporting longest. Says one AP reporter, "I like breaking news. That's one reason I'm with a wire." Top wire service reporters have the best seats at the events that make headlines.

MOST Washington reporters work in the print media, and most print reporters work for newspapers. Newspaper reporting by virtue of its size alone leaves a special stamp on Washington journalism. For example, newspaper reporters ask the most questions at news conferences, thus suggesting an agenda that newsmakers respond to. But mostly the ubiquitous newspaper reporters, many

17. There are certain ironies in reporters' ratings of organizations they would like to work for: newsmagazines, the medium that employs the highest percentage of older writers, are more attractive to the young; specialized publications, the medium with the highest percentage of women reporters, are more attractive to men; network television, the medium that has most increased its percentage of black reporters, is more attractive to whites. One wonders whether journalists find that "the grass is always greener."

in number, unencumbered by elaborate equipment, simply generate so much information from the political solar system that they set the news rhythm of the city.

The information that print reporters generate travels back into the political government (as political actors hear news from reporters or read it on the wire services' printouts) and then out again to the rest of the country via the electronic media. Only in the case of the television networks' Sunday interviews, which are reported in newspapers on slow Mondays, is the process regularly reversed (although print reporters increasingly find cues to the day's news on early morning television programs). Ironically, the prestigious network evening news, most important to the rest of the country, tends to have secondary impact on political Washington, partly because politicians, public officials, and press people rarely get home in time to tune in. (Presidents, for example, generally learn what Walter Cronkite said the evening before from a staff-written summary that arrives with breakfast.) Television's impact comes when constituents and home-office editors close the loop through two other forms of communication, the postal service and the telephone.

Usually, newspapers train reporters in their home offices and then send them to Washington either on permanent assignment or with the expectation of bringing them back to fill managerial posts—more often the former. They supplement their Washington staffs by hiring from other Washington bureaus if they need a specialist or if someone becomes available whose talents cannot be duplicated in the organization. Although one newspaper editor calls promotion from within a "myth" because "the timing is rarely right"— reporters not being ready when a Washington opening develops—organizational maintenance is not breached lightly; another editor explains that he sent a prized statehouse reporter to the Washington bureau only because the reporter otherwise would have left to work for a rival paper.

Of those reporters working for newspapers in Washington, 71 percent are employed by independents and 29 percent by chains. But the percentage working for chain newspaper bureaus will rise, since chains have recently been hiring more reporters, and since more newspapers are becoming group-owned.

A CHAIN is usually defined as two or more daily newspapers in different cities under the same principal ownership or control. However, since this study focuses on the news gatherer in Washington, the reporter is counted as working for an independent newspaper if the bureau serves one newspaper;

a chain bureau serves more than one paper. For example, reporters for the *Washington Post* and the *New York Times* are categorized as working for independents, even though the parent companies own other papers. The distinction also affects chain-owned newspapers that maintain separate Washington bureaus.

While chain operations are often accused of being excessively management-oriented and therefore of being unlikely to spend enough money on bureau personnel, the Washington experience has been exactly the reverse. Newspapers that have been taken over by chains now receive more news from Washington. Many of them were too small—or too cheap—to have had their own Washington correspondents. Others had Washington operations which were merged into the chain bureaus, and some even have kept their own identities.

The strong tug in journalism for local autonomy and the fierce competition between reporters from rival newspapers (even when they have the same ownership) affect the way chains operate in Washington. For instance, Washington reporters for the *Atlanta Constitution* (A.M.) and the *Atlanta Journal* (P.M.), both owned by the Cox organization, are in the same bureau offices, but as far apart as physical space allows. The exclusivity of their stories is carefully protected by the way they transmit copy to Atlanta. When there were two Marshall Field papers in Chicago, the *Sun-Times* and the *Daily News*, they insisted that their adjoining Washington offices have separate entrances despite the fact that they could have had better space if they had not.

Among Washington reporters there is a wide gap between the standings of independent and chain operations: 80 percent of the press corps says they would work for independents, 64 percent for chains; 93 percent of chain reporters would work for independents, but only 68 percent of the reporters on the independents would work for chains. This attitude probably has less to do with the nature of the ownership than with the nature of the papers; chains are often made up of small- and medium-sized newspapers, which carry less weight with news workers and newsmakers.

Certainly the objection to chains cannot be based on evidence that their Washington reporters have less autonomy. On the contrary, as one major chain bureau chief put it, "Having many bosses is having no boss." The bureau for a single newspaper operates under closer editorial control from the home office. Chain newspaper editors defer more to the expertise of their Washington operation. This may be because each paper in the chain has a smaller stake in the Washington bureau; it may reflect less knowledge of national affairs on the part of many of the smaller newspapers' editors; or it may be a direct result of the corporate orientation of some chain managers. Stated bluntly by the bureau chief of a chain that is not held in high repute: "They don't give a shit about news. They're business people. I'm told to proceed on the theory that if you don't hear from us you're doing a great job. I never hear from them. They've never told me to write or not write a story in six years, which is fantastic."

Newspaper chains are accused of being the carpetbaggers of the industry— "on the whole, absentee owners are less sensitive to local nuances," writes Ben H. Bagdikian[18]—but this study finds that their Washington operations devote 40 percent of their staff resources to covering regional news, compared to 16 percent at the independent newspaper bureaus.[19] (The irony, of course, is that chain papers have lower standing in the Washington media partly because of this accent on local news.) Some chain bureaus are almost exclusively in the regional news business; the Thomson Newspapers filed 2,829 stories in 1976, of which only 139 were categorized as national. Even the most prestigious chain bureaus assign substantial portions of their staffs to regional news.

The main chain bureaus—Knight-Ridder, Gannett, Scripps-Howard, Cox, Newhouse, and Copley—have both national and regional staffs, the latter generally having been assigned to Washington by one newspaper in the chain, although in some bureaus a regional reporter covers for several newspapers. While most chains started with a geographic base in one state or bordering states, chains now go after "good buys," no matter the location. As this happens, their regional reporters in Washington are spread over disparate regional beats. The 1978 "Table of Organization" of Gannett—a chain that has worked harder than most toward a rational division of labor— shows that one reporter handles Washington news for Florida, Missouri, and Arizona. The principle of "many bosses is no boss" applies to regional coverage as well—a reporter who handles five papers says he gets fewer home-office requests than a colleague who represents a single paper.

18. *The Information Machines: Their Impact on Men and the Media* (Harper, Torchbooks, 1971), p. 117.

19. On the other hand, independents tend to do more specialist reporting, such as law, regulatory agencies, energy, and particularly economics. Both chains and independents devote similar resources to the traditional beats (White House, Congress, State Department). The number of Washington stories that appear in a newspaper is not related to ownership type, however. One chain newspaper runs a lot of news from Washington, another very little; being part of a chain is not what makes the difference, according to our content analysis of twenty-two newspapers.

The national reporters in the chain bureaus are usually older, more experienced, and better paid than the regional reporters. They are often specialists. Some bureaus are thus in both middle and outer rings: national reporters in the middle ring, regional reporters in the outer ring. This can cause resentment. Says one regional correspondent, "We are overworked and underpaid [in contrast to the national staff]. I'd like the luxury of doing one story a day."

Most regional reporters want to be national reporters. The more ambitious are constantly looking for national stories on their regional beats, often with considerable success. Bureau chiefs do not discourage this practice—they like national stories and in addition see them as good for reporters' morale. However, for those who do not wish to remain in Washington reporting, there is another pattern developing as chains grow larger: the reporter sent to Washington for grooming as an editor of a newspaper. Chain reporters, more than others, say that they look forward to becoming editors someday; reporters for independent papers are more apt to view Washington as a permanent assignment. The increase in chain ownership will create more fluidity, more instability, in the Washington press corps at the same time that it creates a cadre of more sophisticated local editors.

The national staffs at the major chain bureaus devote an increasing portion of time to writing "weekenders," the long articles needed to fill the fat Sunday editions.[20] Such work should be highly attractive, given the complaints about restrictions of time and space, and of being too tied to breaking news. Yet just as chain regional reporters wish to be chain national reporters, chain national reporters want to work for major independent newspapers. The pecking order in Washington newspaper journalism is established by what you do and whom you do it for; whom you do it for comes first.

At least one editor at a large independent paper thinks that bigness itself creates staff morale problems, that Washington reporters turn out more copy than the paper can absorb. The case is rare but not fanciful. A reporter in the editor's bureau says he is now being given more time than he needs or wants to write his stories. He complains, "Sometimes I think I'm working for the *National Geographic*."

Washington newspaper work importantly relates to the size of the bureau. The following precepts apply to both independents and chains unless otherwise noted.

20. Some chains are expanding their papers to seven-day publication schedules. In June 1977 Gannett reported that it had added ten new Sunday editions within the past eighteen months.

A bureau devotes fewer resources to regional news as it grows. In bureaus of three persons or less, all reporters do some regional news, and at least one reporter works almost exclusively on regional stories; bureaus with four to twelve reporters may have two regional reporters, but the other reporters do less regional news; large bureaus, except for the chains, do not add more regional reporters as they expand. H. Finlay Lewis, chief of the three-person *Minneapolis Tribune* staff in Washington, says, "I recently did a survey of stories filed from the bureau over a twenty-month period and discovered that fully two-thirds had a controlling regional or local angle." The *Tribune*, one of the few newspapers with a written statement defining the mission of its Washington bureau, asks reporters to be guided by these questions: "What can I furnish to Upper Midwest readers which will be of special interest or significance to them and which they will not be able to read unless I write it? What can I furnish to the *Tribune* which no wire service or other newspaper is likely to produce?"

A bureau produces more duplicative news as it grows. It sends reporters to beats and events that are also being covered by the wire services and the large newspapers that sell their reportage to client papers. The first beat it adds is the White House, the second, the State Department. It expands away from Congress, the center of regional coverage.

A bureau becomes more internationalist as it grows. This is not only because one of the early additions is a diplomatic correspondent, but also because large bureaus send more Washington-based reporters abroad on assignments. This coincides with the closing of expensive foreign bureaus. While these trips undoubtedly enrich the experiences of Washington journalists, some observers deplore the trend to overseas assignments of only a few months' duration as part of the "erosion" of overseas reportage.[21]

Reporting becomes more specialized as a bureau grows. All reporters in a bureau of three or fewer are generalists; in a six-person bureau, two reporters are specialists; in a ten-person bureau, four reporters are specialists. When a bureau has twenty reporters, only five or six are on general assignments. Most Washington reportage still comes from units that are very small, and most Washington reporters still consider themselves generalists. Yet if the Washington press corps continues to grow (which is not assured, but might, given the rise in group ownership, high profitability, and expanded supplemental news services), more and more stories will be produced by specialists, with the attendant strengths and weaknesses discussed in the next chapter.

21. Barry Rubin, *International News and the American Media* (Sage, 1977), p. 12. See Peter Braestrup, *Big Story* (Doubleday, Anchor Books, 1978), for examples of American media covering the Vietnam War by sending Washington-based correspondents for limited tours.

A bureau hires increasingly from the outside as it grows. This is determined by the needs of a bureau rather than by company personnel policy. Indeed, it works against the best interests of the organization as an organization. Outsiders often get the better jobs. When a bureau wishes to add a reporter to cover the Pentagon or the State Department it is not assured of finding someone with the necessary knowledge in the home office. Promotions to Washington tend to be into the generalist slots, a small percentage of the total in a large bureau and the less desirable assignments. One bureau chief admits that he writes job descriptions for openings (which must be posted at headquarters) so as to effectively exclude persons without Washington experience. Hiring outsiders increases a bureau's autonomy from the home office, which is usually an objective of Washington bureaus. "All things being equal, we will take someone from our organization," says an executive of the *Los Angeles Times*, but things are rarely equal in a Washington bureau of twenty-four professionals. In 1977 only eight reporters in this bureau had been transferred there from the home office. In contrast, all six Washington reporters of the *St. Louis Post-Dispatch* came from St. Louis.

Reporters are not as familiar with the cities in which the newspapers are published as a bureau grows. (This has to be true of reporters in large multipaper bureaus.) Nick Kotz, who worked for the *Des Moines Register* and the *Washington Post*, writes that reporters without a national outlet are "frustrated that their stories lack impact in Washington and are not read by their news sources or friends."[22] Yet this sort of frustration is most seen among those who do not have personal connections with their circulation areas. Reporters in small bureaus usually grew up and still have family in their paper's home cities. This may also compensate for pay disparities between large and small bureaus. For example, though a reporter at the *St. Louis Post-Dispatch* says, "We have a pretty modest pension system," the paper has an excellent record of retaining employees.

It does not necessarily follow, however, that growth leads to staff instability. The large *Los Angeles Times* bureau also has an excellent record of retaining employees.[23] The paper is known for generous economic benefits. A reporter says, "This is a good place to be employed if you get sick."

22. "What the Times and Post Are Missing," *Washington Monthly*, vol. 9 (March 1977), p. 47. Perhaps in support of Kotz's contention, reporters in bureaus that lack a New York or Washington outlet tend to be more active free-lancers.

23. Of the twenty reporters and editors at the *Los Angeles Times*' Washington bureau in 1972, twelve are still there, three have been transferred to Los Angeles, one died, one retired, one runs a family-owned newspaper, one moved overseas when her husband was reassigned and now works for another newspaper. Only one has gone to another Washington news operation.

A *bureau can justify selling its reportage to outside subscribers as it grows.*
A bureau of twenty reporters, and smaller bureaus that band together,
produces sufficient copy to become a supplemental news service.[24] The fees
it charges do not reflect the actual costs of running a bureau. But these
outlays have to be made anyway. Besides deriving a little revenue, the news
services are like a corporation's institutional advertising. A bureau chief talks
of "spreading the image; basically we're not in it for profit." Presumably there
are advantages to the reporters as well, both psychological (being read by
friends around the country) and professional (having senators answer their
calls). Presumably, too, when a bureau emphasizes national news, there are
differences in the stories—what is being covered and how it is being covered.
Yet no bureau chiefs say they assign different types of stories and no reporters
say they write stories differently because they have readers beyond their own
papers' circulation areas. Reporting from large newspaper bureaus is possibly
already so "national" that no changes are necessary.

A *bureau does not become substantially more bureaucratic as it grows.*
This is important to reporters; bureaucratization is what they most wish to
avoid. "Newspapers are our least organized institution," says Julius Duscha,
the director of the Washington Journalism Center—and that is the way news
workers want them to be. Reporters make a fetish of being nonexecutives.
They constantly told our telephone interviewers, always with pride, about the
chaos on their desks. Sitting behind a massive pile of newspaper clippings,
government reports, press releases, and other debris, Richard Dudman, a
respected bureau chief, admits to having "a fear of filing."

Washington bureaus generally add a full-time editor or manager to process
copy and make assignments when the number of reporters reaches a dozen.
Otherwise the burdens of administration fall on the bureau chief, who is
usually elevated from the ranks of reporters and rarely has administrative
experience. In small bureaus, however, the chores are so light that there is
little difference between chiefs and other reporters. James Risser, chief of the
Des Moines Register's bureau (six professionals), estimates that he spends less
than one day a week on office work. Chiefs in larger bureaus, where the
duties are greater, tend to write a weekly column rather than do daily
reporting. (James Wieghart of the *New York Daily News* and Gannett's John

24. Washington bureaus that sell copy include the *New York Times*, the *Washington Post*,
the *Los Angeles Times*, *Newsday*, the *Dallas Times Herald*, the *Chicago Tribune*, the *New York
Daily News*, the *Chicago Sun-Times*, the *Christian Science Monitor*, Knight-Ridder, Newhouse,
Copley, Scripps Howard, and the *Congressional Quarterly*. For a discussion of the hugely
successful Los Angeles Times-Washington Post News Service, see Howard Bray, *The Pillars of
the Post: The Making of a News Empire in Washington* (Norton, 1980), pp. 206–10.

Curley are examples.) Of thirty-two present or former newspaper bureau chiefs interviewed, only two said they had no time for regular writing.[25]

The major nonwriting responsibilities of bureau chiefs come under the heading of "dealing with reporters' problems," often personal. According to Martin F. Nolan, chief of the six-person *Boston Globe* bureau, "I do more stroking than is done at the Westminster Kennel Show." Little time is devoted to making assignments. "Two-thirds of the stories are generated by the reporters themselves," says the chief for a large chain. The bureau chief for an independent paper usually goes over the schedule of stories with a home-office editor each day. Their conversations are conducted in a form of shorthand and seldom take more than a few minutes. Chiefs of large bureaus wire "skeds" to their papers to let them known what stories they can expect. They also have minor office-management duties, such as scheduling vacations and preparing an annual budget. (Two bureau chiefs do not even have budgets.) Occasionally they must represent their companies—giving speeches, attending social events. Rules and regulations are rarely in writing; workers know by tradition what are the permissible limits of behavior.

The typical three-person bureau has a receptionist-secretary; with six reporters, there are two clerical assistants; with twelve reporters, a support staff of three. Beyond this the ratio widens, as clerical hiring almost ceases. The bureaus become sensitive to accusations of empire building. Having secretaries is outside the tradition of newspaper work; even the chiefs at most large bureaus type their own letters and dial their own phone calls. Paradoxically, this admirable restraint in building their own empires eventually works to the disadvantage of the Washington bureaus as their parent organizations grow and make more bureaucratic demands.

WHILE newspapers stress individual enterprise (for example, only in the last few years have they permitted joint by-lines on some stories), and television is forced to be a group enterprise because of its technology, the newsmagazine is designed to be a group enterprise. Henry Luce began with the idea, a weekly journal of coherent narrative. Unlike *Harper's* or the *Atlantic*, *Time*

25. In addition, twenty-eight bureau chiefs filled out questionnaires. Their profile looks much like the older Washington reporter. (Three small papers have chiefs under thirty. No large bureau is headed by a woman.) They are more urban in background and come from the Northeast in slightly larger numbers than the average reporter. While they are a little less likely to have gone to graduate school, they are more likely to have attended "very good" universities. They also are less the product of a journalism curriculum—either as undergraduates (-9 percent) or as graduate students (-17 percent)—another indication that formal journalism studies are not the route to advancement in the Washington press corps.

and *Newsweek* are meant to give the feeling of having been written by one person following some grand design. "Our mission is to provide a perspective on the week," says a *Time* editor. Its Washington bureau reporters feed story ideas and information to the New York headquarters. "But above all," says another *Time* executive, "they feed into a system that maintains narrative control. The key thing is that New York decides and shapes what 'the story' is—the reporter doesn't."

Being part of a centralized operation does not seem to disturb newsmagazine reporters in the same way that it bothers their network television counterparts. The newsmagazines were there first, reporters joined them, rather than the other way around, in full knowledge of the nature of the enterprise. Television reporters, at least the generation that still dominates the Washington bureaus, came to the medium with journalistic expectations shaped by newspaper experience. In both cases, however, there is something about headquarters being in New York that rankles. Viewed from beyond the Hudson and the Potomac, there may not appear to be great cultural differences between the two cities, but one Washington newsmagazine correspondent sees his New York editors as primarily "interested in the kind of social conflict you find in Manhattan." (New York may fault Washington for being equally obsessed with government.)

There are some variations between the operations at *Time* and *Newsweek*, although they do not loom very large to outsiders. Asked to explain the nuances, a former newsmagazine correspondent says, "*Newsweek* is more of a reporter's magazine; *Time* is more of an editor's magazine." Reporters at *Newsweek*, for example, get a form of by-line at the end of a story, while at *Time* they are only occasionally mentioned in the body of a story. *U.S. News & World Report* differs from the others in that its headquarters is in Washington and its stories, on average, are longer and more often the product of a single reporter.

The following is a composite *Time-Newsweek* cycle. On Monday story suggestions are collected from reporters in Washington and sent to New York, New York selects stories and puts a value on each in terms of allocated words, and Washington assigns stories to reporters. From Tuesday to Thursday a winnowing takes place, some stories being cut, some stories gaining importance; room must be made for new developments, and continuous queries go from New York to Washington. On Thursday and Friday reporters prepare material (sometimes as memos, sometimes as stories "written to space," depending in part on how much of the story comes from a reporter's beat), and New York writes or edits the copy based on the "files" that have been submitted. On Saturday reporters check the copy, argue if the facts or the slant differ from their perceptions, and copy goes to the printer. On Monday the magazine appears, and the cycle begins again.

For newsmagazine reporters—who are satisfied with their employment and whose jobs are considered desirable in the Washington press corps— there are obviously important compensations for doing relatively anonymous work in highly structured operations. An older *Time* correspondent talks of good pay, time to write books, expense accounts, travel, and a sabbatical policy. An older writer for *U.S. News & World Report*, a newspaper veteran, prefers "the slower pace." A young *Newsweek* reporter feels a completeness to covering news for a weekly that is not possible when "you have to stop at 4 P.M. and file a story." A younger *U.S. News* reporter enjoys the sense of being part of a group, "the staff meetings each Monday at 9:30, the ME [managing editor] critiquing the issue that has just come out, people making witty and clever remarks, all conducted on a professional level. I have the feeling my superiors know more than I do." The reporters also seem to take pride in the impact of their publications, especially a cover story.

IN ALL types of Washington news organizations most reporters are male, white, urban, and Northeastern. Some organizations, of course, are more urban (network television), some are more male (wire services), some are more white (specialized publications).[26]

The only notable distinction relates to schooling: *the press corps divides sharply along educational lines.* Reporters at the high-prestige organizations (television networks, newsmagazines, newspapers) spend more years in school, usually at more elite schools, less often studying exclusively journalism, than those at low-prestige organizations (radio, wire services). Over half the reporters at high-prestige organizations do some graduate work and a third have graduate degrees. The relationship of high-prestige employer to high educational level is equally true at the chain and independent newspaper bureaus: independents employ 15 percent more reporters with graduate work, 12 percent more reporters with graduate degrees. More chain reporters (+17 percent) major solely in journalism and go to "not selective" colleges (+9 percent).[27] Wire service reporters go to good public universities; magazine

26. See appendix, table 11, "News Organizations: Employment."

27. Chain and independent newspaper reporters in Washington come from the four regions of the country in roughly the same proportions; women do slightly better (+4 percent) in gaining employment in the independent newspapers' bureaus; chain reporters are somewhat more likely (+5 percent) to have urban backgrounds. The five black newspaper reporters in the survey work for independents. More chain reporters (+7 percent) engage in free-lance activities.

and newspaper reporters go to good private schools. Going to the best schools is not mandatory for gaining employment at the top organizations, but it helps.

One might suspect that there would be characteristics that distinguish electronic reporters and print reporters, especially since reporters seldom cross sectors. But this is not the case. Indeed, the profile of a television correspondent is least like that of a radio correspondent and most like that of a magazine correspondent.

Reporters with certain backgrounds are attracted to certain areas of news, regardless of the types of organizations they work for. Reporters compete with other reporters, regardless of the types of organizations they work for. And they share a definition of news, regardless of the types of organizations they work for.

Yet reporters preparing stories for network television, for example, will have to ask themselves, Will they be allowed to film? (Some locations are placed off limits.) Will they be able to film? (Some locations present technical problems.) Will news sources allow themselves to be interviewed on film? (Some information is less useful to television reporters than to print reporters because it is given by sources who wish to be faceless.) Will a story be visually interesting in addition to its news value? Is a story about something that has just happened? (This is a medium mainly devoted to breaking news.) Is this something of interest to the general public? (This is a mass medium.) Is this something that can be explained quickly? (The average story runs 100 seconds.)

The different types of news organizations have different audiences, different missions, different technologies, and different styles of presenting information. Ultimately, then, balanced against the reporters' considerable freedom to choose news, are the requirements imposed by the needs of the organizations that the stories are being written for.

CHAPTER THREE

𝕭𝖊𝖆𝖙𝖘

TRADITIONALLY the assignments given to Washington reporters follow the *United States Government Organizational Manual,* which pigeonholes federal activities into departments and agencies. There is a White House beat, a State Department beat, a Pentagon beat, and so forth, the number depending on how many reporters an organization has. This geographic division of labor—the assignment of reporters to buildings—has advantages. It minimizes jurisdictional disputes between reporters. It is easy to administer. It divides the work load into manageable proportions. These are not inconsequential benefits for operations in which the workers (reporters) constantly strive for autonomy and the managers (bureau chiefs) often dislike managing. "All reporters want to play at the center of the field," says Robert S. Boyd, bureau chief of the Knight-Ridder Newspapers. Geographic beats provide some assurance that the bases will be covered.

Washington news produced beyond the locations that an organization can afford to regularly cover demands a certain flexibility. News organizations may respond to major crises by temporarily shifting personnel or bringing in reporters from other cities, but many organizations, especially big ones, plan for the unexpected by having some reporters without fixed beats—on general assignment.[1]

Another reality of Washington news is that it often does not conform to government organization. Government is a web—everything relates to everything else. Energy policy, for example, is not the exclusive province of the Department of Energy nor urban policy that of the Department of Housing and Urban Development. Therefore, news organizations are increasingly defining beats by substance—what government involves itself in, not the location of its buildings (diplomacy rather than the State Department, economics rather than the Treasury). Whereas geographic beats allow public officials to set the agendas (the game is played on their turf), substantive beats give reporters more control over what the news is and lessen their dependence

1. See chapter 1 for distinction between class A and class B general assignment beats.

47

on one set of sources. The following table shows the distribution of Washington reporters by beat:[2]

Beat	Rank by size	Reporters (percent)
Regional	1	14
Class B general assignment	2	12
Domestic agencies	3	10
Congress	4	8
Class A general assignment	5	8
Economics	6	7
Diplomacy	7	7
White House	8	5
Law	9	5
Politics	10	4
Energy	11	4
Regulatory agencies	12	2
Science	13	2
Other	. . .	10
Unknown	. . .	3

The greatest concentration of reporters cover regional news for newspapers. They are mainly concerned with people and events that have a direct connection with their publications' circulation areas. Most of their time is spent on Capitol Hill. Typically, they are assigned to follow a state's or a city's congressional delegation. Their work includes reporting news of federal grants and federal appointments that are announced through congressional offices, testimony before congressional committees by mayors and other local officials, and, in some cases, compiling a weekly summary of votes by their states' legislators.

More than one-fifth of the press corps work on the regional and congressional beats, combined.[3] Other reporters also make frequent congressional stops, thus making Capitol Hill the dominant location of Washington news gathering. The significance of this becomes apparent when we examine Washington stories in chapter 5. News reflects the vantage point of the news

2. The table records 563 beats held by 476 reporters, with prorating where reporters list more than one assignment. Certain related beats are combined, although they are not always regarded as of equal prestige. Diplomacy includes defense and national security; science includes space; energy includes environment; economics includes business; domestic agencies include agriculture, civil rights, consumer affairs, education, health, labor, transportation, and urban affairs. The congressional beat also encompasses a variety of assignments, some highly prestigious, such as chief Senate correspondent. (Percentages are rounded, so total does not equal 100.)

3. For analysis of the congressional beat, see Robert O. Blanchard, ed., *Congress and the News Media* (Hastings House, 1974).

gatherer; Washington news reflects the perspective of Congress—even though some past measurements fail to detect this.

Washington news is still written largely by generalists: the two biggest beats, regional and class B general assignment, are nonspecialized; they include over a quarter of all reporters. Nearly a third of all reporters have a second beat, which additionally suggests a generalist press corps. Despite the growing number of specialists, most of the reportage from Washington is not produced by substantive "experts."

Back in 1968, Stewart Alsop listed the pecking order of Washington beats as "the White House, the State Department . . . the Hill, and the Defense Department."[4] Other reporters might give somewhat different rankings. These are not simply games press observers play, but are attempts to explain what is reported from Washington and why.

DEVISING a rank order of Washington assignments can best be done by looking at the ages of reporters on each beat. There is an informal seniority system in the news business. Young reporters are usually given the least desirable assignments. As they gather experience, and as openings develop, they transfer to jobs that they find more congenial. The following table, devised by combining three age-related measurements, reflects the hierarchy of beats in Washington today:[5]

High-prestige beats
Diplomacy (1)
Class A general assignment (2)
Law (3)
Politics (4)
White House (5)

Medium-prestige beats
Congress (6)
Science (7)
Energy (8)

Low-prestige beats
Domestic agencies (9)
Regulatory agencies (10)
Economics (11)
Class B general assignment (12)
Regional (13)

4. *The Center* (Popular Library edition, 1968), p. 161.

5. Assignments are ranked (1) by mean age, (2) by the percentage of reporters ages twenty through twenty-nine, and (3) by the gap between the percentages of the youngest and oldest cohorts. Each method produces slightly different results; the exact ranking is less important than the clustering of beats.

Reporters contend that theirs is a young person's profession, but the beats that involve the most fatiguing travel, such as diplomacy and politics, generally are given to senior correspondents. While wear and tear on reporters are not completely irrelevant to assignment, if high levels of energy importantly define newswork (which many reporters believe), then this scale suggests that the prestige of Washington beats is out of line with their physical demands.

As A CHECK against this ranking of beat by age of reporters, reporters were asked "What Washington assignment would you most like to have?" Although nearly 60 percent say, "My present job," those who do indicate a preference for other assignments verify our ranking. It can be assumed that reporters usually want to move to beats of higher prestige and that reporters on prestigious beats are likely to want to remain there. Fourteen of fifteen reporters on the diplomatic beat (high prestige) want to stay where they are; fourteen of twenty reporters on the regional beat (low prestige) want to make a change. (These numbers also show that not all reporters march to the same drummer. While regional reporting ranks at the bottom of the scale, here are six reporters who love this work and would not exchange it for a more prestigious beat.) Only on the law beat is the evidence from interviews not in keeping with the scale. Of eleven reporters (who mostly cover the Supreme Court), only six want the assignment.[6]

Some movement from one beat to another can be explained by reporters wanting to work for a more prestigious news organization. A reporter who covered international relations moved to an influential newspaper: "I said I'd take anything and they gave me economics." Reporters are much less likely to move from a low-prestige beat at a high-prestige organization to a high-prestige beat at a low-prestige organization; however, reporters do move down in organizational prestige to become editors or publishers and leave high-prestige beats to become columnists.

Six factors, in varying proportions, determine the desirability of assignments. First, there is the feeling of specialness that comes from being part of a small, select group. *Exclusivity* is especially strong among reporters on the national political beat; they keep track of potential presidential candidates, travel with those who have the best chance of winning the major party nominations, and then trail the nominees through Election Day. In other years they cover senatorial races, the more important contests for the House

6. The question uncovered other mismatches between reporters and assignments, such as the congressional correspondent who would like to be on the science beat.

of Representatives, and other elections that are thought to have national implications. "We write the rules and we call the game," says a newspaper reporter covering national politics.[7]

There is a high correlation between exclusivity and *travel*. Four of the five high-prestige beats involve a great deal of time on the road; only the law beat is sedentary. The more exotic the travel, the more attractive the beat. As in the game of paper covers rock and scissors cuts papers, Katmandu covers Peoria and Timbuktu cuts Ashtabula—diplomacy outranks politics.

The third factor that makes a beat desirable is *autonomy*. While autonomy relates to age regardless of beat, some assignments are particularly attractive because there is so little "interference" from the home office. The class A general assignment reporter fits this category by definition. When asked what would be the ideal job, a reporter replies, "Total freedom." The freedom to write any story on any turf (class A general assignment) ranks just below the diplomacy beat.

Beats of high *visibility* will always rate near the top in prestige. It is desirable for a reporter to be at a place or covering a subject that consistently generates front-page news or exposure on the television evening news programs. A reporter may be correct in contending that "everything Amy Carter does should not be national news," but much is, and the person doing the story gets the by-line.

Yet the White House, the post of highest visibility, has dropped from first place in Alsop's 1968 ranking to fifth in our computation. Perhaps this reflects who is president.[8] More likely, I think, White House reporting has become increasingly constricting (both for security reasons and because of presidents' attempts to manage the flow of news), while, at the same time, some other beats have become more free-wheeling. Television correspondents give the assignment a higher rating than those who work for newspapers. Two newspaper reporters claim that they moved from Congress to the White House only because it was viewed as a promotion by their employers, and a knowledgeable young newspaper reporter says, "Fewer reporters these days think the White House is the best beat." But cutting remarks about the

7. For analysis of the national political beat, see David S. Broder, "Views of the Press: Political Reporters in Presidential Politics," *Washington Monthly*, vol. 1 (February 1969), pp. 20–33; Martin F. Nolan, "Faust at the Racetrack: Let the Reader Beware," in Frederick Dutton, ed., *Playboy's Election Guide 1972* (Playboy Press, 1972); James M. Perry, *Us & Them: How the Press Covered the 1972 Election* (New York: Clarkson N. Potter, 1973); Lou Cannon, *Reporting: An Inside View* (California Journal Press, 1977), especially chap. 9.

8. See Stephen Hess, "President and Press: The Boredom Factor," *Washington Post*, May 13, 1978.

White House beat, just as about diplomatic correspondents, are often a bit disingenuous: a reporter who denigrated the White House press corps early in the interview later admitted that it was the assignment she preferred. Reporters who say they would like to cover the White House are often at the margins of Washington journalism, with little expectation of getting a White House beat. Perhaps its reputation rises in direct proportion to the reporter's distance from the inner ring.

Beats are also judged by *proximity to power and excitement*, which is not quite the same as visibility in reporters' minds. They seek proximity to powerful and colorful people. Economics produces a lot of news but rates low in the pecking order, partly because Washington reporters define power in political terms, not economic terms, but also because reporters want to cover people who are fun. Politicians are more fun than economists (except perhaps to other economists).

A beat is more desirable if *no documents research* is required. When reporters are asked why they do not want to cover the regulatory agencies, they cite the reliance on documents, which in their minds means endless hours in musty archives, while reporting is supposed to be a constant interchange with colorful, unusual, important people. The prestige rating of the Supreme Court beat is high according to our criteria, but many of these reporters have been trained in the law, so documents research is not onerous and difficult for them. And the beat does have high visibility and proximity to power (though not narrowly defined political power). Yet there is anecdotal evidence that it is not a satisfying assignment. The Supreme Court reporter, in the opinion of one of them, "operates in a vacuum, separated from his sources. He misses the camaraderie that makes conventional political reporting fun. Much time is spent reading briefs. And there are no scoops except in the extraordinary event of a leak."

USING AGE as the means of measuring the prestige of beats may imply that those rising to the top do so only because they stay in the news business longest. But when education is tabulated by beat, the reporters with the most education (with certain exceptions) are also the ones who ultimately get the best assignments.

With almost every reporter having graduated from college, the most useful way to divide above-average and below-average schooling is to measure graduate training. The following table shows the relative educational level of the thirteen beats:

Beat	Reporters with graduate degrees (percent)
Law	64
Regulatory agencies	62
Economics	46
Science	46
White House	41
Diplomacy	36
Class A general assignment	36
Congress	29
Politics	27
Energy	25
Domestic agencies	25
Regional	24
Class B general assignment	20
Average	32

While four of five high-prestige beats are above average in the percentage of reporters holding graduate degrees, it does not follow that all low-prestige beats are below average. Graduate training also correlates with specialization. Above-average education on low-prestige beats indicates that reporters are either specialists or on their way up to high-prestige beats. Below-average education on low-prestige beats profiles reporters more than likely at a dead end.

Those who attend the most selective schools, as noted in the chapter on news organizations, are more apt to work for influential outlets but are not more likely to have prestige assignments. Only two of five high-prestige beats have an above-average percentage of reporters from highly selective institutions: diplomacy (16 percent above the average of the press corps) and politics (12 percent above average).[9]

The heavy attendance of diplomatic reporters at elite schools possibly contributes to the beat's reputation. "State Department reporters are a closed club." "Diplomatic reporters have an inflated idea of their self-importance." One specialist in foreign policy says, "My elitist education makes those around me insecure, so I try to hide it."

However, this is not the reputation of the national political reporters, which suggests that the image of those who cover diplomacy has more to do with a phenomenon described by Russell Baker of the *New York Times*: "The

9. See appendix, table 13, "Beats: Reporters' Traits by Beat."

State Department reporter quickly learns to talk like a fuddy-duddy and to look grave, important, and inscrutable. The Pentagon man always seems to have just come in off maneuvers. . . . and the science specialist becomes detached and takes up pipe smoking."[10] Each beat, according to Baker, has its own personality, which leaves an imprint on the reporter.

Economics is the only beat other than diplomacy that registers above-average for both graduate degrees and attendance at top-ranked schools. This probably reflects rising prestige.[11] If so, the cause is demand rather than changes in the characteristics of the assignment. Heavy criticism of the quality of economics reporting seems to have inspired news organizations to devote more space and money to this field.[12] Salaries for economics reporters are going up. Assuming that this is not a passing fashion, the future economics reporters can be expected to resemble science reporters. (Science ranks seventh, economics eleventh.) Says a science reporter, "We're a very elitist, special breed of cat. We're an entirely different kind of discipline from the usual run-of-the-muck stuff in town. We tend to deal with real people. What they tell you can be put in the bank, unlike most of the information around." But the attitude toward economics among other journalists—who hope someday to cover the White House or politics—is expressed by a young reporter: "Financial news and things like that don't always turn me on. So I tend to think that a lot of reporters skip over it. If I don't read what I should, how can I be surprised if reporters don't want to cover those things?"

What reporters study generally is an indicator of what they will be covering. The science beat, for example, ranks first in the percentage of reporters who were science majors in college, first in reporters with science as a field of graduate study. (Political reporters rank next to last as science undergraduates and last as science graduate students.)

On one beat, however, there is no relationship between field of study and the specialized knowledge most useful in dealing with the substance of the assignment: energy reporters rarely major in science or economics; almost all of them study humanities, liberal arts, or journalism. This can be explained

10. *An American in Washington* (Knopf, 1961), pp. 198–99.

11. While economics is on the rise, there is no indication that the regulatory agency beat, despite being a related subject, will be similarly elevated in the near future. Reporters on the regulatory agency beat have the lowest record of attendance at the elite colleges (19 percent below the press corps average). Another sign is that while women cover economics in roughly the same percentage as their employment in the press corps, they cover the regulatory agencies at twice this rate—and women get the nonprestige assignments.

12. See A. Kent MacDougall, "Business and the Media," *Los Angeles Times*, February 3–8, 1980.

by the newness of the beat. "A year and a half ago," says a reporter for a newspaper chain, "[my bureau] created an energy beat when Congress was about to crank up the energy bill. I have become an 'expert' to the extent that I know the lingo, but this scares me because I don't really understand the technicalities of the subject at all." This veteran reporter has a degree in journalism and considerable overseas experience. Another newspaper reporter says she was "sort of shoved into the energy slot." Her college degree is in political science. She is one of several reporters who were switched from environmental issues to energy issues and appear to be having a hard time adjusting to their new assignment.[13]

Journalism as a course of study bears little relationship to the prestige of the beat. White House and Supreme Court reporters study journalism above the average for the press corps as a whole. State Department reporters are about average, but reporters on the two quintessential Washington beats, politics and class A general assignment, are below average. The same mixed pattern holds for the middle- and low-prestige beats.

THE ASSUMPTION that one of the rewards for reporters' competence is advancement up the ladder of beats does not necessarily take into account differences in the ways they must spend their time at the different locations. To illustrate, we examine reporters' activities on four beats, in descending order of prestige.[14]

The diplomatic beat.[15] In a week that he says is "slightly above the norm, but more or less typical," the network diplomatic correspondent worked sixty-five hours—fifty-five hours for his employer and ten hours for himself (writing a book): Monday, ten; Tuesday, eleven; Wednesday, twelve; Thursday, twelve; Friday, twelve; Saturday, three; Sunday, five. The weekend hours mainly were devoted to preparing for an appearance on a Sunday interview program. He wrote twenty-one stories: sixteen for radio, one for television morning news, four for television evening news. (In a normal week, says his boss, this

13. The newness of the energy beat may account for other characteristics of its composition: fewer than average reporters over fifty years old (-6 percent), more women reporters ($+4$ percent), fewer reporters with graduate training (-12 percent), and fewer graduate degrees (-7 percent).

14. The data in the following sections are drawn from 292 logs kept by reporters for a week. The reporters profiled are not necessarily typical; indeed, many are the busiest members of the press corps. One can assume, however, that other reporters with the same assignments do similar things, even if in slower motion.

15. For analysis of the diplomatic beat, see Bernard G. Cohen, *The Press and Foreign Policy* (Princeton University Press, 1963), and William O. Chittick, *State Department, Press, and Pressure Groups* (Wiley-Interscience, 1970).

reporter would have three stories on the evening news.) He was not, however, covering twenty-one topics. Fourteen of the stories were on a crisis in Africa. Presumably he was also using much of the same material on radio and television.

For the twenty-one stories this correspondent interviewed seventy-two people:

Type of people interviewed	Number of people interviewed
Executive branch civil servant	19
Executive branch political appointee	17
Congressional staff member	12
Foreign diplomat	7
Democratic senator	6
Academic	6
Republican senator	4
Democratic House member	1

The number of executive-branch civil servants interviewed is quite high. Reporters normally do not seek out members of the permanent government to this extent, but the positions of deputy assistant secretary and above, which are held by political appointees in the domestic agencies, are often held by careerists at the State Department. The accent on academics is also unusual, reflecting a closer tie between this reporter and universities than is usually found in the capital. In other respects, these interviews conform to the Washington pattern. There is a major input from Congress, although the reporter's stories are essentially about the executive branch. Typically, too, senators outnumber House members, and Democrats outnumber Republicans during this period when they were the majority party.

Eighteen percent of this reporter's interviews were with government public information officers. This is below the press corps' average (21 percent), but long tenure at the State Department means that he has less need to go through intermediaries.

Sixty-six of the seventy-two interviews (91 percent) were conducted on a background basis, that is, the sources could not be named. This is well above the average for the press corps (25 percent) and even above the average for diplomatic correspondents (64 percent). Diplomats are wont to speak off the record. An embarrassing statement in the press by an official of the government can jeopardize U.S. relations with other nations. The case for granting anonymity to newsmakers in other areas is less strong.

This correspondent did hardly any documents research. For some of his long stories he read State Department press releases, speeches, or newspaper clips. Other stories were based entirely on interviews. For the Sunday program he studied a briefing book compiled by his news organization. (He worries about "shallow TV coverage of major stories and shallow preparation.") In each case he was "primarily responsible for initiating the story," a prerogative he shares with most senior correspondents on major beats.

"As hard as we work in Washington," he says, "it's nothing compared to when we're on a trip. Then we may have to feed satellite at 1 A.M., feed all radio at 2 A.M., finish at 3 or 4, go back to the room for an hour's sleep, and then up for the early morning stakeout. Only the wire services may work as hard."

Another diplomatic correspondent, employed by an influential newspaper, filled out his log during a week when the secretary of state was away. (His paper has two diplomatic reporters, and they rotate trips. This time the other reporter was traveling with the secretary.) The week in Washington was "unusually quiet," says the reporter, but it is worth reconstructing because of the opportunity to see how one veteran spends his time when not under deadline pressure.

There were State Department briefings to be covered (on three of five days), and other "routine operations," such as "keeping in touch with the wires to be alerted to breaking news and see what others are filing." The reporter wrote two hard-news stories, involving nine interviews of which seven were not for attribution. Yet he still worked a forty-eight-hour week, not including two evening seminars (on archeology in the Middle East and press coverage of the Vietnam War).

Primarily he was "keeping up access with sources" and researching two long articles, "in a sense, exclusives," on "U.S. arms sold abroad" and "basic factors in the Middle East." This meant an estimated ten to fifteen telephone calls daily, and the following face-to-face interviews: State Department officials on the Israel and Egypt desks; a legal expert on arms transfers; the head of a foreign central bank (breakfast); the president of a national lobbying organization (lunch); a State Department official in the nuclear nonproliferation field; a State Department official knowledgeable in Cambodian and Vietnamese affairs (breakfast); a staff member of the Senate Foreign Relations Committee; an assistant secretary of state (breakfast); a State Department authority on Soviet and Chinese activities in East Asia; the Japan desk officer at the State Department (concerning a forthcoming visit of Prime Minister Fukuda); an Asian ambassador (lunch).

The week suggests that if given the time a reporter—at least this top reporter—will do a different type of story than usual, either investigative or analytical. But essentially he does not change his technique for gathering information. More time means more interviews. His log shows no greater emphasis on documents than the log of the network reporter who covers breaking news. Apparently it is not the pressure of deadlines that keeps him out of the library.

The Supreme Court beat.[16] Relatively few organizations assign reporters to cover the Supreme Court full time—just the wire services, a handful of prominent newspapers, the television networks, and certain specialized publications. This section draws on the activities of five Supreme Court reporters, three working for newspapers, two for radio and television.

In direct contrast to the diplomatic reporters' heavy emphasis on interviewing, on half of their workdays the Supreme Court reporters conducted no interviews at all. And just as the diplomatic reporters' schedules are markedly different depending on whether the secretary of state is traveling or in Washington, the schedules of the Supreme Court reporters adjust to whether or not it is a "decision week."

The week measured was unusually busy, according to the reporters; they filed fifty-one stories. When the justices were not handing down verdicts, the two broadcast reporters tended to be redeployed to other law-related events, such as a trial, an arraignment, or some activity at the Justice Department. (Of seven stories filed that did not relate to the Supreme Court, five were by the radio-TV correspondents.) Half of all the interviews were for these other stories, and most of the interviewing for Supreme Court stories were also by radio and television reporters.

The Supreme Court makes news by producing written work, and Supreme Court reporters, especially those working for newspapers, cover their beat mostly by reading. One veteran describes his day: "The entire workday was spent preparing case notes for Supreme Court cases due to come up in the following week. Case note preparation merely provides accessible information upon which dictated stories will be based. The materials used were primarily written petitions and briefs of cases before the Supreme Court. The Supreme Court merely provides access to such materials." The work involves "a lot of drudgery," says a newspaper reporter who is new to the beat.

This is a beat on which the same information is made available to all

16. For analysis of the Supreme Court beat, see Chester A. Newland, "Press Coverage of the United States Supreme Court," *Western Political Quarterly*, vol. 17 (March 1964), and David L. Grey, *The Supreme Court and the News Media* (Northwestern University Press, 1968).

reporters at the same time (except for the rare leak). They compete in trying to figure out what the information means. Since the information is in legalese and Court decisions are based on past decisions, news operations increasingly feel that Supreme Court reporters should be lawyers or have some formal training in the law. The three network television correspondents are lawyers. All five reporters hold, collectively, four master's degrees and three law degrees. These last three are reporters who became lawyers rather than lawyers who became reporters. The law degrees are not from the elite institutions and were earned in odd hours after the working day in the news business. On the other hand, two of the master's degrees are from a prestigious school of journalism. (Only one lawyer-reporter in the survey says that he practiced law before going into journalism, and he graduated from a distinguished law school. He is not one of the five discussed here. Also, it should be noted, not all lawyer-reporters in Washington cover the law.)

At the Supreme Court as at the State Department, reporters for the electronic media work longer hours and produce many more stories; the print reporters produce the only analytical pieces; and all reporters work more hours a week than the average in the press corps. Yet, says one Supreme Court reporter, "When my time is spent reading briefs my office doesn't think I'm doing anything."

The White House beat.[17] The White House is the only place where there are demographic changes in the press corps from one administration to another. Some organizations, if they have the appropriate personnel, will assign a reporter from the president's region of the country. For example, shortly after Lyndon Johnson unexpectedly became chief executive, CBS reassigned Texan Dan Rather to Washington and the White House beat.[18] Reporters at the Carter White House were probably somewhat more southern and rural than those who covered Nixon and Ford. The arrival of a new president is also viewed as a good time to rotate reporters, and the White House assignment often goes to the reporter who has traveled with the winning candidate during the campaign.

17. For analysis of the White House beat, see Michael Grossman and Martha Kumar, *Portraying the President: The White House and the News Media* (Johns Hopkins University Press, forthcoming); also see Trudi Osborne, "The White House Press: Let AP Cover the Assassinations," *Washington Monthly*, vol. 8 (February 1977), pp. 16–24; J. Anthony Lukas, "The White House Press 'Club'," *New York Times Magazine*, May 15, 1977; and Eleanor Randolph, "The Secret Pleasures of the White House Press," *Washington Monthly*, vol. 10 (March 1978), pp. 29–35.

18. See Dan Rather, with Micky Herskowitz, *The Camera Never Blinks* (Morrow, 1977), p. 148; also David Halberstam, *The Powers That Be* (Knopf, 1979), p. 435.

The following portrait of a White House correspondent is a composite of three reporters, all men, who work for a wire service, a major newspaper, and a television network. This composite reporter put in a forty-five-hour week and produced ten stories. The television network correspondent again was the most prolific, but he was not nearly in a class with the diplomatic correspondent, perhaps because each network has more reporters sharing the work load at the White House.

The most notable distinction between White House and diplomatic correspondents is the degree to which the former rely on government public information officials. The White House reporter labors in a controlled environment, is limited in the top officials he can interview, dependent on the presidential press secretary's office, and often in attendance at formal or scheduled events. He conducts far fewer interviews than the diplomatic correspondent, and nearly half of them (48 percent) are with the president's press secretary or his staff. Of other key White House officials, only Zbigniew Brzezinski, assistant to the president for national security affairs, was interviewed during the week. Nor were many people outside of the White House interviewed: two Democratic senators (about the Panama Canal Treaty), a "Democratic pollster," and two Democratic House members, one of whom had met with the president. (The logs of three other White House reporters—two working for magazines—list interviews with presidential advisers Stuart Eizenstat, Robert Strauss, and Anne Wexler. However, says a network correspondent, "We don't roam around the halls. You can hardly get into the EOB [Executive Office Building].")

The week of the White House correspondent was spent at briefings in the press room, attending a presidential news conference (out of Washington), going to a presidential speech (in Washington), reporting on the president's meetings with various groups (many with formal debriefings by the participants), and going over White House press releases (such as one on the creation of a coal commission). Documents used were almost always White House transcripts or White House news releases. In short, a White House correspondent sticks close to where the president is, sees him when permitted, and sends forth the word on how the president spends each day. Says the wire service man, "I release reporters to do other things."

The composite White House reporter rates the AP and UPI tickers "extremely important" or "quite important" in his work, especially in keeping up with nonpresidential actions that he may wish to ask a question about during the press secretary's briefings. However, there are other White House reporters whose work is less dependent on breaking news—the magazine writers, a reporter whose paper relies heavily on the wire services to cover the president's daily activities, another who is part of a two-person team.

Compared with reporters on other prestige beats, the White House correspondent has somewhat less leeway in choosing stories. Typically, he writes one major story a week at the request of a news executive in his organization, and in addition may gather material for other reporters' stories. Perhaps because of the high visibility and the interest in the president, but also perhaps because he spends so much time waiting, he is a prolific freelancer.

It is a life with rewards, but also with frustrations. Just about every White House correspondent made a critical comment about the beat: "We're in small quarters with access to only a small number of official people, getting the same information. So we write similar stories and move on the same issues." "The focus is too much on surface events." "Too much pack or herd journalism." "There is too little time spent researching stories." "Too much concentration on the current major story." "Too inbred."

The regional beat.[19] "The bulk of the Washington press corps is made up of localizers," says a regional reporter for several southern newspapers. Mary Kay Quinlan was twenty-seven years old and had been a reporter in the Washington bureau of the *Omaha World-Herald* for four years when she filled in her log, June 12–18, 1978. She was born in Lincoln, Nebraska, received a B.A. in journalism from the University of Nebraska, holds an M.A. in journalism from the University of Maryland, and worked for a year on a newspaper in Rochester, New York.

The *World-Herald*, an independent newspaper with a circulation of 240,000, is the biggest in the state and is read by people in the seven surrounding states. It maintains two reporters in Washington. The bureau chief is Darwin R. Olofson, fifty-six years old, who has been in Washington for the paper for over twenty-five years. His principal responsibility is to cover the Nebraska congressional delegation (three members of the House of Representatives, two senators); Quinlan primarily covers the congressional delegations of the surrounding states, with emphasis on the western edge of Iowa and the northern tier of Kansas. The *World-Herald* relies on AP, UPI, the New York Times News Service, and the Los Angeles Times-Washington Post News Service for its other Washington news.

19. For more on the regional beat, see Ben H. Bagdikian, "Diggers and Toilers," *Columbia Journalism Review*, vol. 2 (Summer 1963), pp. 36–38; Edmund B. Lambeth and John A. Byrne, "Pipelines from Washington," *Columbia Journalism Review*, vol. 17 (May–June 1978), pp. 52–55; Mick Rood, "Washington's Other Reporters," *Washington Post Magazine*, June 18, 1978.

Quinlan later said that those who read her log would "think I did a stupid, ridiculous, trivial type of work. It's not impressive, and has no status in many people's minds. But I enjoy it. People in Nebraska have the same right to know what's going on as people who read the *New York Times*." Regional reporter Quinlan worked a forty-five-hour week spread over five days. She wrote fifteen stories, a total of 5,085 words, an average story length of 339 words. The longest story (890 words) is a compilation of "how Nebraska and western Iowa congressmen voted." Her shortest story (40 words) reports the awarding of a federal grant to the Nebraska Arts Council. Other stories: BILL WOULD PREVENT FORCED TRUCKERS' PAYOFFS—475 words about a House subcommittee hearing, chaired by an Iowa congresswoman, on a bill to prevent truckers from making payoffs to freight handlers in order to get perishable goods unloaded at warehouses; GASOHOL COMMISSION TOLD: HEED INTENT OF CONGRESS—350 words about the Nebraska congressional delegation urging faster development of alcohol fuels made from agricultural products; N.U. SEEKING FEDERAL RESEARCH FUNDS—390 words about University of Nebraska educators in Washington to meet with various federal officials; LAW SAID TO HINDER DOCTOR AIDES—320 words about the contention of the chancellor of the University of Nebraska Medical Center that state law, promoted by the medical profession, hinders the expanded use of paramedics; O'NEILL PLAN FACES BATTLE FOR FUNDING—510 words, on page 1, about an impending vote in the House of Representatives on funding for a Nebraska irrigation project, and the conflict between Nebraska and Iowa members of Congress.

Quinlan's stories were printed with "no editing or cuts." In this regard, her experience is similar to that of her prestigious and older brethren on the diplomatic, Supreme Court, and White House beats, all of whom report that editing and cutting are not serious problems. However, there is a significant difference in how the stories are "played"—only one of her pieces was on the front page; much of the material by reporters on the other three beats was prominently displayed.

Quinlan describes her week as "fairly typical." It is also typical of most regional reporters in that she did a lot of short articles and that the articles were based on few interviews (an average of 2.6 for each story listed above). Her week is unusual for a regional reporter in that almost half of her stories are unrelated to Congress. Much more typical is the day spent by a regional reporter for a newspaper chain who wrote twelve versions of "House rejects farm bill," each with an insert on "how local congressmen voted with quotes." Also, Quinlan is not typical in that only one of her stories is not regional (a short article on a speech by economist Herbert Stein). Other regional reporters stray more often into the national arena.

In one respect, Quinlan's work is more difficult than some regional beats. She reports for a state that has not been noted for its national political figures since William Jennings Bryan and George W. Norris. Unlike those who write for readers in Minnesota or California, she writes without colorful or powerful politicians to draw upon.

She was not involved in other activities for her newspaper, social events or speechmaking. She did no free-lance work. "Many folks at home believe Washington reporting is more glamorous than it is—Georgetown parties, hobnobbing with the great and the near-great. It's not," she says.

FOUR BEATS—diplomacy, law, White House, regional—each part of Washington journalism: the intensive reliance on interviews at the State Department and on documents at the Supreme Court; the closed environment at the White House and the open access on Capitol Hill. Each calls for a different body of knowledge to explain what is going on, but each relies on the same skills of communicating.

"You can't be a generalist anymore. Government has grown too big and complex," says a newspaper reporter specializing in diplomacy.[20] Some subjects, such as energy, have even become "mega beats," requiring a technical understanding of several disciplines.[21] Still, the tradition of journalism and the lure for many who make it their work is otherwise:

A good reporter can become an instant expert on anything. . . . Ignorance can be good because you then ask the same questions as the home viewers. . . . You've got to know a little bit about everything because nothing works in a vacuum. . . . There is value in coming to a story with your innocence untarnished.

A majority of the reporters on the diplomacy and law beats consider themselves specialists; the majority on the White House and regional beats consider themselves generalists. But not all reporters agree on these distinctions. Says a television correspondent at the White House, "It would be next to impossible for a generalist to walk into the White House and listen to a press conference and know whether or not Carter was changing his position. I'm a specialist on White House affairs." On the other hand, a newspaper reporter emphatically denies that having a law degree makes him a specialist.

Based solely on what they wish to call themselves, the Washington news

20. Specialist reporters favor more specialization in Washington journalism; generalists are even more strongly in favor of a generalist press corps, which recalls Miles' Law: "Where you stand depends on where you sit" (formulated by Rufus Miles, a former assistant secretary for administration of the Department of Health, Education, and Welfare).

21. The phrase *mega beat* is borrowed from Edmund B. Lambeth, "Perceived Influence of the Press on Energy Policy Making," *Journalism Quarterly*, vol. 55 (Spring 1978), p. 72.

corps is composed of 39 percent specialists and 61 percent generalists. The percentage of specialists would be less if reporters used standard definitions of expertise based on formal training and other professional characteristics. But in journalism, says a television reporter, "A generalist will become a specialist if he stays on the beat." Says a newspaper reporter, "[In Washington], being a specialist means knowing a lot of people in your field, rather than knowing an awful lot about what you're writing about." (This was not meant critically.)

The looseness of the specialist label can be seen by looking at what reporters read. One characteristic of specialists in a profession is that they consume a steady diet of the periodical "literature." Yet on only two beats— diplomacy and science—does a majority of the reporters list among the magazines read regularly the specialized publications that are related to assignments. Economics reporters, although they cover primarily economic policy, not business, read *Business Week, Fortune,* and *Forbes,* but not journals of economics. Less than a quarter of the law beat reporters regularly reads law journals.

Still, no matter how imprecise their definitions are, a majority of those interviewed agree that Washington journalism is moving toward greater specialization. A basic problem in creating a more specialized news-gathering system is that the beats reporters agree require specialization are not the beats reporters want to be on (except for diplomacy). For example, 84 percent think regulatory agencies are not sufficiently covered and 51 percent think this is a serious problem.[22] Yet there is no evidence to suggest that reporters are prevented from doing this work. Says a reporter for a major regional newspaper, "It's drudgery. We've hired four or five people to cover regulatory agencies and they switch to another beat as soon as possible." News of government regulatory actions is often buried in the documents, is often best understood by those at the lower reaches in the agencies, is often what one reporter calls esoterica. Notes a reporter who says she spends 90 percent of her time covering this field, "There are no 'breakfasts with the secretary.' Interviews with the big names don't do much good. You have to go to the docket room and sift." Another reporter says he is a "specialist on garbage. . . . Trash isn't well enough covered." (The "garbage man" gets more calls

22. Thirty-five percent of the reporters blame editors for the lack of regulatory agency coverage, 21 percent blame the news system, 15 percent blame themselves, 13 percent blame the regulatory agencies, and 7 percent blame readers or listeners. "Congress makes itself easy to cover, the regulatory agencies don't." "They keep adding agencies." "The readers aren't interested." "The editors bury the stories." There is probably truth in all the accusations.

a week from readers than many famous journalists.) But this is not what most reporters went into journalism to do.

Thus Washington is covered by a generalist press corps in transition, and some reporters are uneasy about what the future holds for them. There are those who fear that specialization limits their prospects for promotion. Says a magazine writer, "Being a specialist is not an attractive career option because you get pigeonholed and don't advance." Beyond self-interest, reporters worry that specialization leads to *tunnel vision* (cited by 31 percent of the critics), narrowing perspective and ignoring overall implications; *elitism* (25 percent), catering to small groups and writing over the heads of the public; *co-optation* (23 percent), becoming beholden to sources and functioning as their "cheering section"; *poor writing* (15 percent), the excessive use of jargon and being less understandable than need be; and *bias* (6 percent), turning reporters into advocates for programs, people, or a point of view. (This listing does not imply that generalists have no concerns about their own brand of journalism. A southern regional reporter notes, "We can fake a lot of things, and we do.")

In response to the media's perceived need for greater specialization in Washington coverage, some organizations have been experimenting with hiring experts from outside the ranks of journalists. They report that the results so far are not encouraging. In the opinion of an editor whose newspaper is noted for business reporting, "It's easier to make a reporter into an economist than an economist into a reporter." A television news executive feels it is even harder "to find experts with on-camera ability." He says his network was not able to hire a physician for a medicine/science slot after hundreds of interviews.[23]

The consequences of a more specialized press corps cannot be fully anticipated. (Certainly the news industry is making no effort to anticipate them.) But the future will be different if only because specialists are different. Besides having more university training, they are older and more often come from the Northeast than the average Washington reporter. There are fewer black specialist reporters. Thus the demographic profile of a more specialized Washington press corps may be even less of a reflection of the population than is currently the case.

This survey shows that specialists are considerably more likely than

23. An exception to these experiences is described by the then editor of the *National Journal*, John F. Burby, who claims success in training young Ph.D.s as reporters. See his "Academics: First-rate Reporters," *Nieman Reports*, vol. 27 (Fall 1973), pp. 26–27.

generalists to form their circle of closest friends from persons outside of journalism and that specialists are more satisfied in their work. Will there be less pack journalism or is pack journalism a by-product of something other than fraternal relationships among reporters? Will higher levels of job satisfaction mean that reporters will remain in the news business longer? Indeed, is less personnel turnover good or bad in terms of how the news is reported from Washington? (We return to these questions in the concluding chapter.)

One firm judgment, however, is offered: the greater the reporter's expert knowledge, the greater the reporter's freedom from editorial supervision.[24] Surprisingly, given the power attributed to press lords and the like, much of the data collected for this study suggests a very high degree of autonomy among reporters in the Washington news corps. Editors already indicate that considerable deference is paid to their national reporters simply because they are experts on "Washington." Sorting the work load into beats that require greater specialization will further move the point of initiation away from the home offices.

24. Some reporters contend otherwise, claiming that specialists are more at the mercy of editors, "a rather trendy bunch," says a science writer, who adds, "They cool off on a subject and then they kill it. Space news was killed by editors, although the public is still interested." "They think race relations stories are passé," says a specialist in race relations, "but they're not."

CHAPTER FOUR

𝔗𝔯𝔞𝔦𝔱𝔰

"WE REALLY do represent society. We should be an accurate reflection of society." So thinks a television network correspondent, who is forty-one years old and grew up in a suburb of a large East Coast city. He graduated from an elite private college in the South with a degree in business administration. After starting in journalism at a local television station, he spent most of his career with the network that assigned him to Washington. He has had one overseas post. We do not know his politics, although we know he believes that reporters are "generally liberals."

"Most reporters [in Washington] are liberal, college-educated, male, white, and middle class," says a newspaper correspondent. She is thirty years old and grew up in two western cities. She graduated from a state university of limited prestige, where she majored in journalism and political science. She spent her first year in journalism at a wire service, but has since been employed by an independent newspaper that assigned her to Washington after an overseas post. Politically she claims to be "more middle-of-the-road than the rest."

These two reporters are among the 476 (38 percent of those covering national government for American commercial news organizations) who provided information about themselves. Their backgrounds, collectively, form a profile of the Washington news corps.

AT A TIME when there are two male professionals in the United States for each female professional, the Washington news corps consists of four male reporters for each female reporter—the same ratio found in a national survey of journalists conducted in 1971. Since this study was made in 1978, it can be assumed that the hiring of female reporters in Washington lags behind the rest of the United States by seven years.

The most striking demographic difference between Washington's male and female reporters is that the women as a group are considerably younger. They are twice as likely as men to be between twenty and twenty-nine years old. Nearly 84 percent of women reporters are under forty years of age; 52 percent of male reporters are under forty. Otherwise, what is notable is that the reporters, regardless of gender, come from similar backgrounds.[1]

Most of the women, however, are employed at the least prestigious places, which also pay the least. When the Washington press is divided into influential and noninfluential organizations, 28 percent of the women and 38 percent of the men work for the influentials. In broadcast journalism, for example, women's jobs are still mostly in radio and local television, although they are making gains at the networks. The percentage of women reporters is modest at the wire services and at newspapers, especially chain operations. They hold their own at magazines and do well at regional news services.

A number of older women got their start in Washington at the regional news services, writing local-angle stories for small newspapers that were not in a position to maintain their own bureaus; others first covered regional news for the wire services. As the regional news business declines, there are fewer of these entry level jobs. Instead the "place" for women in Washington journalism has become the specialized publications. Nearly one of three women reporters works for the specialized press; the comparable figure for men is one in six.

A twenty-seven-year-old woman is the junior member of a two-person bureau; her assignment is to cover engineering for five specialized publications. When she got a master's degree in journalism her dream was to be a Washington reporter for a daily newspaper. The only job available was on a weekly in upstate New York. After several years she was making more than the starting salary on a daily; she then came to Washington as the press secretary to the congressman from her district, which led to her present job. She says she can't get a job on a daily now because she hasn't had this type of experience. She thinks she should have taken a pay cut to work in daily journalism. While happy in her present job, she no longer believes she will ever be a Washington newspaper reporter.

She is right, statistically, at least. Of 194 reporters who gave detailed

1. Washington women reporters are more likely than their male counterparts to grow up in the South, less likely to come from the Northeast. They come from the North Central and the West in about the same proportions. Women are slightly less urban in background and slightly more likely to have spent their childhoods in one location. The percentage of male and female reporters that attended graduate school is the same, but men have many more graduate degrees (probably because women reporters are younger and likely to be still completing university training). The percentage of men and women attending private colleges and universities is very similar; the men's schools, however, are rated more selective. Women, both as undergraduates and graduate students, are more often journalism majors; men more often major in liberal arts or humanities; the percentage for science and technology is about the same.

information on the journalism jobs they have had in Washington, less than 3 percent of those who switched employers went from a specialized publication to a newspaper. The specialized press is easier to get into, but it is not a good place to move up from. A publisher of nine newsletters employs five women reporters: one recently graduated from college with a journalism degree, two were hired from congressional offices, two came from other specialized publications. The pattern is mostly to upgrade employment within the specialized field. The women reporters who did make the transition to daily journalism cover economics, an area with few qualified writers. As the managing editor of a major newsmagazine notes, "We now pay premium to get economics reporters, even more than for foreign policy experts." But even with that advantage, it took nine years for one of the women to land a job at the Washington bureau of a leading newspaper.

Women not only work for the lower prestige organizations, they also get the lower prestige assignments. Three highly desirable beats—diplomacy, politics, and the presidency—have the lowest percentage of women (although all three television networks have had female reporters at the White House in recent years). The three beats with the highest percentage of women are regulatory agencies, domestic agencies, and law. A woman reporter at the Supreme Court says, "People at my bureau say, 'I'm sure glad you're doing that, I wouldn't want to.' "

When general assignment beats are divided into class A and class B, with the former signifying that reporters can pick their own stories, women have half as many class A assignments as their percentage in the press corps and exceed their class B "quota" by 5 percent. The only other assignment that women get in higher than "average" numbers is energy, a beat so new and so quickly formed it resembles a pickup team in sandlot baseball. It is not that women reporters do not get beats that are important or beats that generate a good deal of news, merely that they get the beats that men do not want.

Women are assigned to cover the domestic departments at a rate almost double their percentage of the press corps. This is where the "women's issues" are. Covering women's issues is a matter of some ambivalence among women reporters. A writer for a major independent newspaper says, "As the only woman in a twelve-person bureau, I don't want to be typed as a women's issues reporter. But no one else will do those stories. [The male reporters] might not refuse to do them, but they don't generate them on their own." A young reporter in a small newspaper bureau claims she "has purposely avoided covering events which might be characterized as women's stories." But others note that such issues as the Equal Rights Amendment attract them as women and as reporters. A newspaper reporter from a small bureau complains that the reason such stories do not receive more attention is "the scarcity of female reporters." An older reporter in a large chain bureau claims that "women's issues produce enough important news to justify a full-time beat."

There is a difference between social issues and social events. The latter is how the powerful in Washington entertain each other. This survey, however, is about those who cover national government, and these women are deeply angered when their editors blur the distinction. "They still think that if Mrs. Carter has a tea a woman should cover it," says a wire service reporter. "But it's much better now than it used to be."

Themes of improvement and satisfaction are often repeated by the older women. A reporter in her sixties recalls, "There used to be a definite bias against women. [My organization] didn't send any women overseas and was 'fussy' about which beats to give us. This has changed enormously." A well-known journalist, now in her mid-forties, says, "I have achieved so much more in life than I ever expected to when I was growing up."

Younger women are more apt to talk about the pressure of their jobs. A radio reporter, after three years in Washington, says, "It's rough. It really is. Everything you do has to be to prove yourself, every newscast is like an audition. Of course, this is true of any field in which women are proving themselves. You're conscious of it all the time."

Journalism has had the reputation of being a macho profession, hip flask and egg on the vest. Yet the complaint is seldom made by women reporters in Washington. One veteran, working for a very large specialized publication, believes "the problem is mostly with younger male colleagues. They feel threatened by women. Older men aren't threatened. They just say, 'She thinks like a man.' "

Complaints relate to Washington more than to journalism. After her first year in the capital, an experienced newspaper reporter claims, "Washington is the most sexist place I've ever lived." When covering the government, says a reporter for a specialized newspaper, "There's the 'ole boy network,' and if you aren't a boy you don't get in. There just aren't enough women in high places out there to keep the tips flowing." Some women find certain beats particularly uncongenial. "Labor is very male-dominated, with traditional macho attitudes." "Covering finance you're not taken as seriously." Women working for prestige operations report fewer problems. "They identify you with your organization, not your gender."

Women and men of the same age working for the same type of organization have similar aspirations, although women are more motivated to get into television work and less interested in administrative positions. They are four times more likely than men to want to host a "talk" program or be an "anchor"; half as likely to want to be an editor. Despite seldom getting the best beats or working for the best organizations, Washington's women reporters rate themselves as highly satisfied with their jobs as their male colleagues.

IN THE UNITED STATES 38 percent of minority employees on daily newspapers are not black. But in Washington's national news corps, *black* is virtually synonymous with *minority*. Just one minority respondent in this survey is not black, making other minority groups—Asians, Chicanos, Latinos, native Americans—collectively, one person removed from nonexistent.

At the same time, there are so few blacks in Washington national journalism (less than 4 percent) that the statistics—when arranged in units as small as beats—become quite shaky.

Robert Maynard, the former ombudsman of the *Washington Post* and a leader in the education of minority journalists, contends that "demand for minority news employees has been in direct proportion to conflagration." This survey supports his position, showing modest black hiring after the falloff in civil rights protests. Of twenty-nine types of Washington stories, those about civil rights are tied with veterans' affairs for twenty-third place. With fewer news events directly relating to blacks, news organizations apparently think they have less need for black reporters—or perhaps are less aware of the absence of blacks on their staffs. When a group of Hanafi Muslims took over three Washington buildings in March 1977, holding 133 hostages, *Time* magazine had to bring a black reporter from San Francisco since it had no black reporter permanently assigned to the capital.

The gap between minority percentages in the Washington news corps and in journalism throughout the nation probably has widened during the last few years. Most blacks are new to the news business and Washington is not a place of entry level employment. The prevailing attitude is expressed by the bureau chief of a newspaper chain: "I wanted a black to cover the White House, but I couldn't find one in the organization. Hiring a black reporter from the outside would have been an insult to the blacks [in the organization]. We have promising talent, but they're not yet ready. The worst thing would have been to pick somebody who turned out to be a disaster."

Minority journalists, then, are caught in a squeeze when seeking Washington jobs: there is no demand for specialists in issues of concern to minorities, and there are few new openings for generalists. Hiring is now mostly for replacement; the least experienced are the most adversely affected.

A committee of the American Society of Newspaper Editors argues that "the intensification of the feminist movement directly on the heels of the civil rights movement has been both a reason and an excuse for a lessening of effort to recruit minority newspeople."[2] In Washington the hiring of female reporters has continued at a steady pace, unlike that of black reporters. A result of social movements in collision is the "two-fer" phenomenon, filling two minority slots with one job. Twenty percent of white reporters in Washington are female; 53 percent of black reporters are female. Ten percent of female reporters are black; .02 percent of male reporters are black. Black female reporters, when interviewed, more often stress their blackness than their femaleness. A black woman leader suggests that this is because black women view feminism as a white movement.

Just as white women break into the Washington news corps by way of specialized publications, blacks (both women and men) enter through broadcast journalism, most notably at low-prestige radio and local television, but increasingly also at the television networks. Fifty-six percent of the black reporters are employed by the electronic media; only 6 percent work for specialized publications. Blacks fare badly at regional news services, chain-owned newspapers, and wire services; they fare somewhat better at independent newspapers and magazines. But because of employment by the television networks and certain major newspapers, blacks slightly exceed whites in their respective percentages at the influential organizations.

One difference between female and black employment in Washington journalism is that, while females are being hired at a slow-but-steady rate and blacks at a minute-and-diminishing rate, blacks are more apt to be found in high-prestige organizations with high-prestige assignments. It is not true, as a black woman radio reporter contends, that "women and blacks get off-the-wall assignments." Blacks do quite well on the White House and congressional beats; less well on the diplomatic and class A general assignment beats. Politics is the only prestige beat on which blacks do badly. Along with white women, they are overrepresented on class B general assignment and domestic agencies beats (the latter being the location of black issues as well as women's issues). Unlike white women, however, blacks do not get assigned to cover law, economics, regulatory agencies, energy, or regional news. The assign-

2. American Society of Newspaper Editors, "Report of the ASNE Committee on Minorities, April 4, 1978," p. 4. Also see Vernon Jarrett, "A Record That Can Be Improved," *Chicago Tribune*, April 12, 1978.

ments given blacks reflect their relatively greater presence in broadcasting, which, more than the print media, concentrate resources at the major institutions that are the elite beats.

The age patterns for blacks and women are similar, but for blacks the tilt is even more toward youth. Nearly 53 percent of black reporters are in their twenties; only 6 percent are over forty years old. (Black women reporters, on average, are older than black men reporters.) The educational attainment of black and white reporters is impressive: 48 percent of white reporters and 41 percent of black reporters have some graduate school training; 33 percent of the whites and 29 percent of the blacks hold graduate degrees. Blacks more often go to public universities; whites, at a ratio of three to one, attend more selective schools. Blacks are almost twice as likely to specialize in journalism as undergraduates and graduate students.[3]

Strong motivation, especially among the very young, is obvious when talking with black journalists. From a radio reporter: "I'm so driving that I haven't let being black or being female or being young hinder me." From a television reporter: "They [her network] don't trust me much. But it's 'cause I'm new. So they give me soft stuff to cover. It doesn't bother me, I can get on camera a lot." From a reporter on a prestige newspaper: "I'm aggressive. I expect people to treat me well, and I have few problems." The few complaints—at least expressed to white interviewers—came from the older reporters.

"If you're going to operate in some wonderland, you can say that your background doesn't color your story," contends a black male reporter. Many white reporters claim that who they are will not affect what they write about or how they cover a story. Not so, say most black reporters. "It does make a difference in my coverage that I'm a black," says a woman who works for a Middle West newspaper. "My sources will be different. In covering the Rules Committee, for example, I'll interview Shirley Chisholm. I know her, while a white reporter might not. On an economics story I'll be interested in how it affects minority business. Minority business keeps up the tax base in the cities, minority business restores pride, minority business is good. So minority business is important to me, although it's only a small matter in the total economy."

White bureau chiefs often feel uncomfortable about assigning black

3. Black reporters in Washington are overwhelmingly from the South; all other regions are underrepresented. They are more urban in background than white reporters, and more apt to have spent their childhoods in one location. They are also almost three times as likely to have had jobs in government at some point in their careers.

reporters to cover civil rights. They would prefer to think that they could be color-blind in parceling out stories. But black reporters do not display the ambivalence of some white women reporters, torn between professional and personal interests. Quite the contrary. As one interviewer noted about a newspaper reporter, "He mostly covers race relations. This is what he wants to do. He doesn't feel that covering black issues stereotypes him." Reporters working for outlets with predominantly black audiences express a special sense of mission and are among those most satisfied with their jobs.

ONLY ONE of five Washington reporters is in their twenties. The capital is not the place to start a career in newswork. (In the rest of the nation, one out of three journalists are in their twenties.) It might appear that the high percentage of women and blacks among younger Washington reporters presages an eventual change in the composition of its news corps. Actuarially, older reporters (heavily white and male) die or retire first; younger reporters (more heavily black and female) become their replacements. *Any such straight-line projection is wrong.* Young Washington reporters are not tomorrow's Walter Cronkites and Walter Lippmanns. Most young reporters are working in radio, nonnetwork television, specialized publications, and regional news services. The pattern is to spend a journalism career in the same news sector; reporters in Washington move from newspaper to newspaper or from television network to television network. There are exceptions, of course, but young reporters on specialized publications are most apt to become old editors on specialized publications, or to leave journalism. The future superstars, when in their twenties, are serving apprenticeships in Nashville at the *Tennessean* or at owned-and-operated stations of the television networks.

Young Washington reporters can be divided into three unequal groups. The largest will quit journalism sooner than later. The percentage is merely guesswork, but it may be close to the 61 percent who say there is "some work other than journalism that [they] would like to do someday." Many of these people see reporting as a diverting way to spend a few years until something better comes along. A young college graduate (with a minor in journalism) gets her first job on a specialized publication; two years later she contemplates returning to school for advanced training in health care administration. A young man abstracts court decisions for another specialized publication; he is going to law school at night and will quit his job when he gets his degree.

It is possible that competition for jobs in journalism eventually will shrink the category of the least committed. Wayne Kelley, executive editor of

Congressional Quarterly, says, "When Dave Broder came to Washington [in the 1950s], *CQ* was the only place he could get a job, but now we can attract people with four or five years' experience, and [a young] Broder wouldn't be hired here." The major specialized journals—despite low salaries—are already finding that they are no longer limited to hiring recent college graduates.

The second group of young reporters will have careers outside the mainstream of mass journalism, often doing highly technical writing and editing. One young woman has been working for four years at a newsletter on housing. She likes the idea that she is reporting on a subject that "newspapers don't cover well." She likes the feedback from an audience that, although small, is vitally interested in what she produces. She feels part of a community. She says with pride, "Recently I went to the funeral of an important Hill staffer [in my field]. Other than his family, there weren't ten people there I didn't know." Such reporters feel the lure of better paying mid-career jobs in government and industry. But as specialized publications become highly profitable, and as they increasingly change from "ma and pa" operations to chain or even conglomerate ownership, salaries can be expected to rise in order to create a more stable and efficient personnel structure. It also may be that as the need for specialists increases, young reporters will have the opportunity to move from trade to mass journalism. Moreover, specialists will be most in demand at the most important bureaus.

The smallest group of young Washington reporters is composed of a handful of people in their twenties who have already found positions at the major organizations, plus others whose backgrounds, particularly educational achievements, suggest they will use the toehold in Washington to start an upward climb. A 27-year-old reporter with a degree in history from one of the most selective eastern colleges and a master of arts in international relations from another elite institution covered congressional delegations for a struggling regional news service for a year and a half. She is now on the next rung, a magazine with small circulation and prominent readership that has served other reporters as a way into major news organizations. It is not irrelevant that she studied history and international relations; those who major in journalism as undergraduates are least likely to end up in the best organizations. The woman with degrees in history and international relations says she would like to work for the *Wall Street Journal* "on foreign assignment or in international economics." At the other extreme, 14 percent of her age group, when asked what job in journalism they "would like best to have someday," respond that they are content with their present job. Those entering the fast track appear to dream more grandly.

"The younger the reporter," says an older reporter, "the more likely he is to have a sympathy for the left of center." This statement is more a reflection upon the older reporter's own youth than careful observation of today's young reporters. Says a twenty-four-year-old writer for a specialized newsletter, in a typical comment, "I'm not a very political person." And when political sympathies are evident they are not necessarily more liberal. "I'm a laissez-faire capitalist," says a twenty-six-year-old radio reporter with three years of Washington experience. In contrast, a forty-year-old radio reporter, in Washington for eighteen years, says, "It's best for the country if the news is reported with a liberal bias." Find young reporters who read *Mother Jones* and you find they also read *Time* and *Newsweek*. But it is hard to find young reporters in the Washington press corps reading *Mother Jones*.

Far from being on a political rampart, young reporters are mostly interested in their careers. Their university training, both as undergraduate and graduate students, is above the news corps' average in science and technology and journalism, well below average in liberal arts and humanities. Furthermore, when they complete their formal education, they will have more years of career-directed schooling than their elders.

The system tests the acolytes. While young reporters do not work harder or longer hours, they are given the least interesting work. They are on general assignments or covering the activities of the local member of Congress. Rarely will young reporters be found at the White House or the State Department. They write lots of little stories (an average of almost nine a week, nearly three more than the average produced by reporters in their forties); of all age groups they spend the most time on stories that do not pan out, have the least opportunity to travel (nearly half of them did not leave Washington on assignment in the past year), have the highest number of disagreements with their editors (and a greater ratio of them about story requests from the home office), and they rate their jobs least satisfying.

Yet journalism organizations are highly paternalistic; if young reporters survive, they will have to work hard to get fired.

MORE Washington reporters are in their thirties (38 percent) than in any other age cohort. The increase over the number in their twenties largely reflects transfers from other places; over half of all Washington reporters are sent there by their employers. Hiring an outsider for such a coveted assignment is a tacit admission that the organization lacks talent, and it lowers morale among those who are passed over. One Washington newspaper reporter hired from the outside says that her friends in the home office told her, "Stay out of the newsroom or wear a bullet-proof vest."

Transferring reporters in their thirties to Washington is most pronounced at national news organizations, such as the wire services and television networks. Nearly 53 percent of Associated Press and United Press International reporters, and 60 percent of correspondents at the television networks, arrive in the capital at this time in their lives. They have proved themselves and earned promotion. The more national the news operation, the more it looks on Washington as the premier assignment. Foreign beats may have a certain lure for short periods or for certain types of people, but a Washington dateline is the greatest guarantee that a reporter's work will appear regularly and prominently.

While reporters entering their thirties are turning up at the prominent news organizations, they are also dropping out at the lower prestige places.[4] The result of these separate movements—they are not the same people—is that 14 percent of those in their twenties and 41 percent of those in their thirties work for the influentials.

This age group is starting to get the better beats. Assignment to the White House is up sharply. Regional reporting drops sharply.[5] Reporters do even better on the diplomatic beat as they grow older, and eventually they will have greater freedom to choose their own stories, but the biggest improvement in assignments comes as they move from their twenties to their thirties.

Dissatisfaction with their jobs declines sharply, from 22 percent to 13 percent. Reporters in their thirties have fewer disagreements with their editors over home-office requests for stories. They are more likely to argue over story placement and story length. Some are beginning to think about becoming editors themselves, particularly if they work for newspaper chains.[6]

This is not to imply that these reporters give much thought to their professional futures. "I never think about it," says a thirty-year-old writer for a weekly newsmagazine. Partly this is because they are so busy. Almost a third spend a month or more a year out of Washington on assignment (compared with 7 percent of reporters in their twenties). During a typical week in 1978, a thirty-seven-year-old reporter for a Middle West newspaper

4. Four percent fewer reporters in their thirties than in their twenties work at the regional news services, 6 percent fewer at nonnetwork television, 8 percent fewer at specialized publications, and 10 percent fewer in radio. Three percent more work at general circulation magazines and wire services, 8 percent more at television networks, and 15 percent more at newspapers.

5. Of reporters covering the president, 7 percent are in their twenties and 59 percent are in their thirties. Regional reporting ranks second of all assignments given to reporters in their twenties and eleventh (of thirteen beats) for reporters in their thirties.

6. Twenty-seven percent of all reporters in their thirties want to be editors. Four percent of the reporters in their thirties are bureau chiefs.

is in California looking into the meaning of Proposition 13, a thirty-two-year-old television network reporter is traveling with Mrs. Carter in Costa Rica, a thirty-eight-year-old reporter for an Eastern newspaper is preparing himself for a trip to Africa. Recalling the legwork of a long career in journalism, a newspaper reporter nearing retirement says, "The ideal age for a Washington reporter is twenty-eight to thirty-eight."

Reporters in their thirties in 1978 were in college during the years of civil rights and Vietnam War protests. Do they carry the seeds of social activism into journalism? According to two thirty-nine-year-old reporters, "You are apt to become a reporter because you have a social conscience" and "[Washington reportage today] reflects the tenor of the universities in the early sixties." But these are minority opinions. Very few of the hundreds of interviewees hint at any special sense of social mission. One newspaper reporter (aged thirty) sees himself as "changing from a sixties lefty to a seventies moderate." He talks wistfully about wanting to "cover baseball," hardly a radical's pastime. A television network reporter (aged thirty-two) notes that he and his colleagues are now "middle class and damned well off." He makes the point to illustrate that this is not a news corps of campus liberals. If these reporters are masking their zeal because it is bad form to seem too involved, they are doing a good job.

Yet the overall impression is not that the news is reported as if the sixties never existed: the residue of that era appears to be distrust of public institutions and politicians, rather than social activism. "One bunch of bastards is just as bad as another," says a reporter (aged thirty) at a leading newspaper. The event of the sixties with the greatest impact on news gathering, at least measured by how frequently it is mentioned, is Watergate. This was a Washington story, and Washington reporters did more than cover it, they were participants.

THE QUARTER of the Washington news corps between forty and forty-nine years old are, to use a baseball term, the power hitters. This is the decade when the experience line (on the upgrade) crosses the energy line (on the downgrade). At the point where the lines intersect, reporters write the longest stories and, by a small margin, work the most hours. Those in their forties average a forty-four-hour workweek, an hour more than those in their thirties.

These reporters are more likely than younger reporters to be bureau chiefs and much more likely to want to become bureau chiefs. They are also considerably less likely to request foreign assignments. Being a foreign correspondent is clearly a job that appeals to the young; 93 percent of those who want to go overseas are under forty years of age.

The greatest percentage of reporters doing free-lance work are in their forties. These writers often have above-average educations (in terms of graduate training and the selectivity of the schools they attended) and often are on important beats (such as diplomacy). They are less likely than their age peers to work for television networks, more likely to work for chain newspapers. After-hours journalism is produced by a combination of opportunity and the need for money or recognition (money being cited as the reason twice as often as recognition).

The migration into Washington journalism, except at magazines and the TV networks, almost stops when reporters reach their forties. Reporters in these years are overrepresented on newspapers and television networks, underrepresented at other types of organizations. As for assignments, the percentage of reporters between forty and forty-nine years old has risen in diplomacy and politics, declined in domestic agencies, regional reporting, class B general assignments, economics, the White House, and law.

Job satisfaction has some correlation with age except for a small jump in the dissatisfaction level among reporters in their forties. One forty-six-year-old reporter for a newspaper chain (twenty-three years in journalism, ten years in Washington) now sees the amount of news in newspapers as "how much is needed to wrap around the grocery ads." Yet he does not look for work with another news organization ("This is one of the best"); there is no other city that is better for the journalist ("I'd have to take a huge pay cut"); and there is no other type of work that has an appeal ("at least not enough to walk out the door"). He can expect to feel better about his work after fifty.

AMONG Washington reporters who have lived beyond a half century (16 percent of the press corps), there must be a special satisfaction in the example of Richard L. Strout. Strout was eighty years old in 1978. He was born in Brooklyn, New York, and went to Harvard University, majoring in English and government in his undergraduate years and in economics for his master of arts. He has covered Washington for the *Christian Science Monitor* since 1924, and has written the TRB column in the *New Republic* since 1943.

During a week in April 1978, Strout filed five newspaper stories (600 words each) and the magazine column (1,100 words). The stories deal with the economy, illegal Mexican immigration, the Panama Canal Treaty, the Bakke case, and sales of arms to the Middle East. The column is a "light essay" on E. B. White. He produced 4,100 words in four nine-hour days and one six-hour day—a forty-two-hour workweek. He also did a radio broadcast. The week, he notes, is "typical."

Strout at eighty "lopes around the capital like an eager twenty-year-old making good on his first assignment from the city editor," writes former *Newsweek* columnist Kenneth G. Crawford.[7] Journalism, it is often contended, is a young person's work. But a Richard Strout reminds us—as do a Margot Fonteyn and a Satchel Paige—that there are people who seem to have special glands.

His background also reminds us that older Washington reporters are as often the product of the most selective universities as the youngest Washington reporters and as likely to have graduate degrees as reporters in their thirties. They are the least likely to have majored in journalism.

The high educational attainment of Washington journalists over fifty years old can be attributed partly to the GI Bill, but many Washington reporters of Strout's generation were also college graduates. When Leo Rosten surveyed them in 1935–36, he found that 65 out of 127 (51 percent) had college degrees and another 36 (28 percent) had some college training.[8] The news business may have an affection for the legend of the high-school dropout who starts in journalism by filling pastepots for the copy editors, but this has not been the dominant career pattern in the United States for a long time, especially in Washington.[9]

The older Washington reporter is almost nonexistent at nonnetwork television and radio.[10] But general circulation magazines, with nearly 10 percent of the news corps, employ over 15 percent of the older reporters. The attractiveness of magazine work is in part the longer deadline (although reporters at magazines still complain that they do not have enough time to write), and in part the opportunity to do interpretive writing. At a specialized publication, the older journalist is likely to be an editor or the owner.

At newspapers, 10 percent of the older journalists are bureau chiefs. Their duties—which they usually look upon with distaste and often admit doing

7. "Crossing Paths of Journalism with Richard Strout," *Christian Science Monitor*, March 24, 1978.

8. Leo C. Rosten, *The Washington Correspondents* (1937; reprint ed., Arno Press, 1974), p. 159.

9. Haynes Johnson, of the *Washington Post*, says that in the 1930s his father, Malcolm, a New York reporter and a Pulitzer Prize winner, lectured on "the myth of *The Front Page*," challenging the stereotype of the lower class, ill-educated journalist depicted in the popular Ben Hecht–Charles MacArthur play. A number of Washington reporters come from journalism families. These second generation reporters usually work for other organizations than the ones that employed their parents. While connections may well be helpful, primarily in gaining entry level jobs, parental example is the main legacy—these are the children of *successful* journalists. There is little nepotism in journalism: editors do not hire their children (although publishers do).

10. For a discussion of the older correspondents at the television networks, see chapter 2.

badly—are not really onerous. Except at the large bureaus, few spend more than one day a week doing them. The bureau chief continues to write, probably a weekly column, and has a few outside activities—speechmaking, attendance at professional conferences or annual meetings with other executives in the organization, entertaining "visiting firemen."

Twenty years ago, says an editor, his newspaper used its Washington bureau as a "high-level dumping ground for those who weren't going any place in the organization." There are Washington bureaus where some think this is still the case. A reporter for a large chain feels his bureau has a considerable "geriatrics problem."

But the vast majority of news organizations look at Washington as the place to send their best, and most older journalists who continue as reporters do so because it is what they most enjoy. "I've been an editor and a bureau chief and I like reporting better," says a magazine correspondent. More than 63 percent of the Washington reporters over fifty years old think that the "best job" in journalism is their "present job" (compared to 40 percent of those in the forty through forty-nine-year age group); nearly half of the older Washington reporters give the highest satisfaction rating to their work, and less than 10 percent report being dissatisfied. Dissatisfied older reporters tend to have once held assignments of greater importance, often at large organizations that can afford to put them on the shelf until they retire.

Those over fifty years old have seen much change in Washington journalism. They are not always pleased with the change. They have seen television assume a dominant place in the distribution of news. Young print reporters were not around in the days before presidential news conferences were televised live, and, if they take notice at all, appear to be somewhat envious of the celebrity status of their television competitors. But the older newspaper reporter often looks upon television as an unruly child who gets too much attention from the grown-ups. The written word is serious, pictures are for those who can't read. "Policymakers," says a national correspondent for an important newspaper chain, "vastly overrate the influence of electronic journalism and cater to it because they do not understand that most citizens make up their minds on the basis of what they read." (The slight irony is that of all age groups, Washington reporters over fifty years old watch the most television news—over five programs a week, one program more than reporters in their twenties.)

Older reporters are also more apt to lament what one of them calls the trivialization of news. "Suddenly the whole industry is nuts on personality pieces," says another. This is not a complaint of younger reporters who are more likely to say that "the journalist has to try to attract the reader's attention" or "news comes alive when you talk about personalities." It is not that youth is frivolous and their elders are solemn—some young reporters in Washington are very solemn and older reporters are usually not noticeably so. Rather, there is something that rubs off on reporters after spending years observing great events, a certain propriety of form when writing about affairs of state or the gross national product.

There are older reporters who voice concern over the sourness they now see in the relations between government and press. Investigative journalism "has gone too far." A reporter who came to Washington in 1963 says, "People now are writing stories when they shouldn't be. I hate to think what would have happened if we'd been wrong on Watergate; we violated a lot of tenets." Perhaps it is just that the older reporter is slowing down; for example, they work at least three hours less a week than reporters in their forties. But they also may have a less adversarial conception of their job. "News gathering is not meant to be an eternal struggle between reporter and newsmaker," says a senior woman correspondent. "Each could better understand the other's motivation and thus create a more honest and open climate between them."

Yet, without exception, older journalists feel the news corps does a better job now than when they came to Washington. "On balance, a superb job," says the editor of a large specialized publication. A Washington reporter since 1944 recalls, "When I started, there were many of the older writers who had such profound prejudices that it greatly biased the copy they would write. . . . They rejected everything that smacked of liberalism and their editors applauded. These old mossbacks covered Washington as they saw it, and they saw it with a jaundiced eye and made no pretense of impartiality."

"The press is more sophisticated and less partisan than fifty years ago," concludes Richard Strout.

JOURNALISM could be characterized as a semiprofession. Practitioners need not have a license, certification, or special academic training, yet Washington reporters are increasingly the products of good universities and hold graduate degrees.

There are still a few people around who went from high school to copy boy to reporter, such as Grant Dillman, the UPI bureau chief. And Robert J. Donovan, retired from journalism since 1977 after a distinguished career that included running the Washington bureaus of the *New York Herald Tribune* and the *Los Angeles Times*, tells how he got his first job: "The editor [at the *Herald Tribune*] was a grisly old Texan. . . . There he was stuck with all these Yalies. When I told him I hadn't been to college, a light came into his eyes. He hired me."[11] But each year there are fewer journalists in the Donovan-Dillman tradition; reporters under thirty years old are three times more likely to have a college degree than those over fifty.

In 1936, 51 percent of Washington reporters were college graduates; in 1961, 81 percent; and in 1978, 93 percent. Only 6 percent had graduate degrees in 1936; 20 percent in 1961; and 33 percent in 1978.[12] While these figures reflect more schooling throughout the population, they also indicate that Washington reporters have had a lot of formal education for a long time.

Whereas doctors and lawyers are schooled in their chosen fields, reporters do not necessarily study journalism. Nearly 52 percent of the Washington press corps have no university journalism course work. Of those who complete advanced programs, less than half (48 percent) get their graduate degrees in journalism. Nor is the rise in the number of journalism majors in the United States—from 11,390 in 1960 to 64,151 in 1975[13]—reflected among the younger Washington reporters: 26 percent of reporters in their twenties, 27 percent in their thirties, and 22 percent in their forties have journalism degrees.

Instead, Washington reporters overwhelmingly major in the humanities or liberal arts (62 percent). Over 6 percent earn doctorates or law degrees. It is a press corps with a broad background of academic interests, although not one well versed in the natural sciences.

Washington reporters go to very good colleges and universities, nearly 35 percent to schools in the two most selective categories based on the percentage of applicants accepted, test scores of recent freshman classes, and other scholastic measurements. Only 20 percent go to schools not ranked "selective".[14] Their graduate schools are even more selective—by nearly 7 percent. The majority of highly selective schools are private institutions; 57 percent of the press corps are from private colleges and universities, which also suggests something about the socioeconomic standing of Washington reporters.

Those going to highly selective undergraduate colleges are more likely to study humanities or liberal arts; those who major in journalism as under-

11. Karen De Witt, "For Robert Donovan, Journalist, Missing Yale Didn't Hurt," *Washington Post*, August 24, 1977.

12. Rosten, *The Washington Correspondents*, pp. 159–60; and William L. Rivers, "The Correspondents after 25 Years," *Columbia Journalism Review*, vol. 1 (Spring 1962), p. 6.

13. Ben H. Bagdikian, "Woodstein U," *Atlantic*, March 1977, p. 82.

14. James Cass and Max Birnbaum, *Comparative Guide to American Colleges*, 8th ed. (Harper and Row, 1977), pp. 742–46.

graduates are not as likely to go to selective schools. Graduate work in journalism, on the other hand, tends to be at selective schools, such as Columbia and Northwestern.

The Washington reporters most likely to be educated at highly selective schools are those in their forties, those from the Northeast, those with urban backgrounds, and those who work for influential news organizations. Reporters from the South and West and those who grew up in rural areas are more likely to go to colleges ranked "not selective."

Those with graduate degrees also tend to be from the Northeast and to be in their forties. The highest percentage of reporters with graduate degrees work for independent newspapers, and cover law, regulatory agencies, and science.

The authors of the 1971 survey of U.S. journalists conclude that "there is little consensus among practitioners in the field as to what type of college training best prepares one for employment in the news media."[15] Their data suggest that journalists think some field other than the one they majored in would have been more useful. Only a third of the journalism majors, for example, recommend their own discipline for those "entering news media today."[16]

Washington reporters, on the other hand, overwhelmingly feel their education has been useful, no matter what they studied. Only 23 percent express dissatisfaction with their formal schooling. Of course, compared with journalists outside Washington, their education is deeper and more various. The political science undergraduate may have a graduate degree in journalism; the economics undergraduate may have gone on to law school. These are the people for whom education has paid off: news gatherers who believe they work in the most important news-making city in the world.

The few who are dissatisfied with their education have not done less well in their profession. Nor are they distinguished by place of employment (although they are overrepresented on specialized publications); nor by their course of study (although dissatisfied journalism majors tend to be the most vocal); nor by age (although those under forty years old are more dissatisfied than those over forty).

What does stand out is that the vast majority disappointed with their education did not go to top-flight institutions. Also, statements of dissatisfaction often reflect an awkward mesh between education and job. A reporter

15. John W. C. Johnstone, Edward J. Slawski, and William W. Bowman, *The News People* (University of Illinois Press, 1976), p. 40.
16. Ibid., p. 205.

for the *Journal of Commerce* who majored in languages wishes he had studied economics; a reporter for *Science Service* says she should have taken more science courses.

When reporters mention subjects they wish they had studied, economics leads the list (35 percent), followed by political science and history (18 percent each).[17] "Economics and finance would have better prepared me to understand government," says a thirty-year-old reporter, a journalism major who works for a newspaper chain. "Nothing is more useful in understanding the interrelationship of government and public and international events than a good grasp of economics." Few reporters express an interest in course work that would have improved writing skills—nor do editors look for it when hiring. The use of language does not appear to be much on the minds of Washington journalists.

WHEN the regional backgrounds of Washington reporters—where they grew up combined with where they went to college—are matched against the distribution of the U.S. population, the Northeast is heavily overrepresented (and numerically the greatest). The North Central (or Middle West) holds its own. The South, which includes Maryland, Delaware, and the District of Columbia, is slightly underrepresented. Most of the East's gain comes at the West's expense.

Region	Washington reporters (percent)	U.S. population (percent)
Northeast	38	23
North Central	27	27
South	26	32
West	9	18

Moreover, there is only the most modest evidence that the Washington press corps reflects the shifting of the population from the snow belt to the sun belt, that is, from the Northeast and North Central to the South and West. Comparing backgrounds of reporters over forty years old with those under forty, the sun belt picks up less than 5 percent among the younger reporters, and these are entirely from the South; the West actually loses ground. (Part of the gain from the South may be a response to having two Southerners, Lyndon Johnson and Jimmy Carter, as president.) Reporters in

17. Among the other subjects that reporters said they would like to have studied: English (10 percent), journalism (9 percent), medicine or science (5 percent), and law (4 percent).

their twenties from the Northeast are actually nearly 5 percent above the average for the press corps. One reason Westerners are underrepresented may be that they resist transfer to Washington; at least that is what a California newspaper editor says of the young reporters on his staff. On the other hand, a young reporter from the Middle West, who enjoyed covering his state legislature, remarks that "it took me fourteen seconds to say yes" to a less desirable assignment in Washington.

Reporters from the Northeast are far more apt to be educated at highly selective private universities than reporters from the other regions. Nearly 58 percent went to the "best" schools, almost three times the percentage of North Central reporters. Nearly half of the Northeast reporters attended private institutions, more than twice the figure for the North Central. The gap is even wider between the Northeast and the South and West. Reporters from the Northeast are also most likely to be male and white. Black reporters are overwhelmingly from the South, and women reporters more often come from the South than from any other region.

Journalists from the Northeast, though the most numerous, do not necessarily work for the most influential news organizations. They are most often employed at regional news services, television stations, chain newspapers, and specialized publications. There are other relationships between reporters' regional background and their news organizations. Many newspaper reporters grew up in the Middle West (a fact that Rosten also noted in 1936).[18] In contrast, the electronic media appeal to Southerners. The South is especially dominant in radio, but has above average representation in television also—both local stations and the networks. Apparently a Southern accent is no handicap in broadcasting.

Certain regions are almost synonymous with certain beats: the Northeast and diplomacy (+ 21 percent); the North Central and politics (+ 13 percent); the South and domestic agencies (+ 11 percent). Those who cover Congress come closest to approximating the U.S. population by region.[19]

The backgrounds of Washington reporters are more urban than the U.S. population. In 1978, 67 percent of the American people lived in a standard metropolitan statistical area (SMSA), but 75 percent of the Washington journalists grew up in these areas. However, some of these areas may not

18. *Washington Correspondents*, pp. 156–57.

19. Thirty-eight percent of all Washington reporters and 59 percent of the diplomatic reporters are from the Northeast; 27 percent of all Washington reporters and 40 percent of those on the political beat are from the North Central; 26 percent of all Washington reporters and 37 percent of those covering domestic agencies are from the South.

have been SMSAs when the reporters were growing up there. Thus this comparison probably somewhat overrepresents the urban background of the Washington press corps. Moreover, the differences between Washington reporters with urban and rural histories are very slight.

"SOME reporters feel that there is a political bias in the Washington news corps. Do you agree?" Of the 178 Washington reporters who answered this question, 51 percent agree and 49 percent disagree. Those in agreement were then asked to describe the bias. *Liberal* said 96 percent, *conservative* said 1 percent.

Yet something curious happens when the reporters are asked to characterize their own politics and to say whether they agree with the prevailing political views of the Washington news corps.

Forty-two percent consider themselves liberal, 39 percent say they are middle-of-the-road, and 19 percent identify themselves as conservative. Forty-six percent feel their views are in conformity with the politics of the press corps, 7 percent are more liberal, and 47 *percent claim they are more conservative.*

In other words, those reporters, a majority, who think there is a political bias in the Washington news corps overwhelmingly agree that the bias is liberal, yet most do not think of themselves as liberals. Indeed, almost half feel that they are to the political right of their colleagues. It is reminiscent of a famous Thomas Nast cartoon in which Boss Tweed and his henchmen are arranged in a circle, each pointing an accusing finger at his neighbor. The caption reads, " 'Twas him." Washington reporters seem to be similarly arrayed: the press corps is liberal, but not me. " 'Tis him."

How can a press corps in which the majority of its members consider themselves middle-of-the-road or conservative be perceived by the majority of its members as liberal? The answer may be that perception has not caught up with reality. In the past the Washington press was liberal; a variety of data bears this out.[20] Thus Washington reporters may still accept a stereotype of the news corps that is no longer accurate.

Or, as some reporters contend, the stereotype reflects a few news gatherers who work for certain influential organizations and are assigned to certain

20. In 1936, Rosten found Washington correspondents 13 percent less Republican and more Democratic than the nation (*Washington Correspondents*, p. 191). Also see Rivers, "The Correspondents after 25 Years," p. 5; and National Press Club, Professional Relations Committee, "The Press Covers Government: the Nixon Years from 1969 to Watergate," prepared by American University, Department of Communication (Washington, D.C.: National Press Club, 1973), p. 6.

highly visible beats. "Only the big guns are really the liberals," says a reporter for a newspaper chain. "The bulk of the news corps consists of regional reporters who are of all political persuasions." A diplomatic correspondent says, "They're more conservative at the Pentagon." Reporters who work for the influential outlets are 10 percent more likely to view the press as liberal, and television network correspondents are the most likely to see a liberal bias among Washington reporters. At the same time, these reporters are more apt than those who work for noninfluential organizations to characterize their own politics as middle-of-the-road.

A liberal bias is built into the nature of Washington news gathering. Reporters' objectives are to get good stories on their beats—that is, things need to happen in government and on the national level for them to benefit in the competition with other reporters at other places. Government action (as opposed to private-sector action) and federal action (as opposed to state and local action) coincide with traditional liberal tenets. (A Texas editor makes the same point about his state capital reporters having an Austin bias; others comment that foreign correspondents can be expected to have an internationalist bias.)

On the other hand, the "big" stories—the ones that win prizes—are often exposés, and some reporters contend that this biases them "against whomever is in office." The newspaper-chain reporter who made this observation says he was "a Democrat when Nixon was in office, and a Republican now [that Carter is president]." In terms of Washington reporters' professional interests, it might be said they are for government and against officeholders. However, this attitude must be tempered by the fact that they need officeholders to get good stories.

Finally, some reporters believe there is a bias in favor of political figures who are "good copy." They can be counted on to provide colorful quotations and are more fun to cover. "But it's not because of their politics," adds a magazine writer, although many of the colorful politicians have been liberals in recent years.[21]

Liberal and *conservative* are, at any rate, mushy words in our political lexicon. One person's (or region's) liberal may be another's conservative. While the Washington news corps should have a fairly consistent view of what these words mean in American politics, the value of these data are as

21. For a view that the bias is "stylistic," that Washington reporters are attracted to a political style "that could be characterized as elegant, urbane, cosmopolitan," see Stephen Hess comment in "Has the Press Done a Job on Nixon?" *Columbia Journalism Review*, vol. 12 (January–February 1974), p. 55.

self-perceptions, rather than for what they might tell us about where reporters stand on any particular issue.

Cross-tabulations by ideology (on such questions as how well the news media are informing the public, how good a job is being done by the reporter's own bureau, and disagreements with the home office), show virtually no differences between reporters who claim to be liberals and reporters who claim to be conservatives. There are slight differences between conservatives and liberals as a group and all others—the independents, those in the middle of the road, and those who give no response. Those who admit to an ideology react more strongly, but on professional matters they react in the same direction.

"Few reporters have strongly held political beliefs," a thirty-six-year-old reporter for a newspaper chain concludes. The statement is echoed in many other interviews. A thirty-year-old reporter, who gave very thoughtful responses to our questions, notes, "I am astonished at how many reporters here have no political views. Perhaps the majority I know do not have a clear ideological leaning and are genuinely uncertain in their own minds of which way they would swing on a variety of cutting-edge issues." Hardly any Washington reporters say they participate in community activities, and some make a point of saying they do not vote. In several cases they volunteer this information to show how far they go to be objective, but professionalism is not always cited as the reason for nonparticipation.

An apolitical press corps in Washington, if this is the case, looks like a strange finding. One might expect that those covering the national government would have a deep interest in political ideas. Instead, the lure of Washington seems to be otherwise; the attraction perhaps is to excitement and powerful personalities. It also may be that the gap in prestige, salary, and public attention between Washington reporting jobs and other reporting jobs is so great that even journalists who prefer to do some other type of reporting feel that they must come to Washington to get ahead.[22]

Also, the impression from the interviews is that the reporters, although feeling "out of touch" with the American people, often hold views—even about themselves—that are similar to those widely held in the country: "I

22. This survey does not attempt to measure affluence and includes no question on income. Notable, however, is that the *Washington Post* and the Newspaper Guild signed a new contract in 1979 that included a $596-a-week "top minimum," the highest in the country. And for an experienced Washington reporter at a leading newspaper there are extras—merit raises and cost-of-living increases. Austin H. Kiplinger places "senior Washington newspeople" in "the top 5 percent of salary earnees in the U.S." *Washington Now* (Harper and Row, 1975), p. 264.

vote for the candidate, not the party." "There's no difference between the parties." "The press reflects what's popular in academic circles." "Washington reporters are part of an eastern elitist establishment."

Do REPORTERS who work for certain important news organizations have markedly different characteristics than other Washington reporters? The influentials—that 36 percent of the press corps defined as the inner ring in chapter 2—are the television networks, the weekly newsmagazines, the wire services, and the four newspapers most often read by Washington journalists, namely the *Washington Post*, the *New York Times*, the *Washington Star*, and the *Wall Street Journal*.

The Washington press corps as a whole is not young, not female, and not black; it is heavily from the Northeast and well educated. Reporters of the inner ring are even less young, less likely to be female, more schooled, more likely to be from the Northeast. They are, however, more likely to be black than the press corps in general, reflecting minority hiring at the *Post* and the television networks.

Reporters at the influentials attend more selective universities and are more likely as undergraduates to major in liberal arts or humanities. Journalism tends to be the field of study of those who work for the noninfluentials. (However, those who work for influentials and noninfluentials do about the same amount of graduate work in journalism.)

The two groups of reporters are most apart in age. Influential organizations are generally national and thus their reporters come to Washington after a period of testing at other locations. Less than 8 percent of reporters at the influentials are in their twenties.

The differences between the workers for the influential and noninfluential news organizations are not statistically very significant. But the direction of the differences is noteworthy. If there is an average Washington reporter and an average American, they do not look like each other; the average influential Washington reporter looks even less like the average American.

CHAPTER FIVE

Stories

SUNDAY through Saturday, April 9–15, 1978, may not be a typical week in Washington—no seven days ever being exactly like another—but the week contains all the standard elements and events that constitute "news" in the nation's capital.

During this week the Senate debates the Panama Canal treaties; the House of Representatives defeats an emergency agriculture bill, and farmers protest the defeat in public demonstrations; the president of the United States delivers a speech on inflation, calling on government, industry, and labor to "sacrifice for the common good," and holds a news conference; the American Society of Newspaper Editors meets in Washington; the president of Rumania is also in town; half of the cabinet testifies before congressional committees, four cabinet members appearing twice; a presidential commission recommends a major overhaul of the military pension system; Ralph Nader issues a statement; the secretary of Health, Education, and Welfare has unkind words for the tobacco industry, and the Tobacco Institute responds in kind; the Civil Aeronautics Board proposes a new fare structure for domestic airlines; the Consumer Product Safety Commission expresses concern about certain children's toys; Senate and House leaders go to the White House to try to work out a compromise energy bill; a Korean-born businessman is found guilty in Federal District Court of conspiring to bribe congressmen; a federal grand jury returns an indictment against a former director of the FBI; and investigative reporters are looking into the private business dealings of the Speaker of the House.

Nothing terribly exceptional happens. There are no serious eruptions in the world causing reporters to rush to the State Department or the White House. No single congressional hearing dominates the news. Nor is this week in the midst of either a presidential campaign or Washington's August doldrums. In other words, it is a good week to look at the news media's coverage of Washington—reporters are in their usual places, more or less, noting the events that pass before them. The following analysis is based on the Washington stories that appeared in twenty-two newspapers and on the evening news programs of the three television networks.[1]

What is most immediately apparent is that news of Washington dominates the media's attention. Forty-five percent of the reporters seen on camera during the network evening news programs are based in Washington; twelve of fifteen lead stories come from Washington.[2] This might be expected of national outlets that need not make room for local stories and that can operate more economically by concentrating resources so heavily in one location. But it is startlingly true of newspapers as well. Collectively, these papers use 1,050,515 words by Washington reporters during the week,[3] over twelve Washington stories a day on average for each newspaper.[4]

1. The newspapers were chosen to represent a mix of regions, ownership arrangements, political affiliations, readership, and competitive situations. Daily circulations range from almost two million for the *New York Daily News* to less than 30,000 for the *Anniston [Alabama] Star*. Thirteen papers list their political affiliation in *Editor & Publisher Year Book* as independent, four lean Democratic, four lean Republican or conservative, and another does not say. The papers come from sixteen states. Seven are published in the Northeast, seven in the South (including Baltimore and Washington, D.C.), four in the North Central states, and four in the West. Twelve of the papers appear in the morning, eight are evening papers, two have A.M. and P.M. editions. Eight of the papers are represented in Washington by chain bureaus, thirteen have their own Washington bureaus. Three newspapers have no competition in their cities, four have direct competition, fifteen have indirect competition from a paper published on a different time cycle (although in six cases both papers have the same ownership). The percentages in this chapter that do not specifically refer to newspapers or television also include the Washington output of *Newsweek*.

2. The percentages for the television networks refer to the half-hour programs that are heard in Washington at either 6:30 or 7 P.M. on Mondays through Fridays. Thus the figures on television—just as those on newspapers (see footnote 3)—do not represent the total Washington news that is available from the mass media.

3. Vast as it is, this number is not the total words that these papers print about Washington. No stories under two inches in length were coded. (Inclusion of these very short pieces would undoubtedly boost the percentage of wire service copy.) No editorials were coded. No Sunday magazine sections were coded. Stories from Washington that do not concern government were not coded. (For example, the *Buffalo News* ran a Washington dateline story about an expert on antiques, and a Washington-based reporter for the *Chicago Sun-Times* did a travel article on Colonial Williamsburg.) The survey does not include stories about the federal government that were written locally, such as coverage of a speech by a congressman in his district or a federal contract announced through a regional office. Nor were nationally syndicated Washington columns coded. (This would have added approximately 217,000 words.) However, syndicated columns written by a member of a newspaper's Washington bureau were coded for the writer's own paper. For example, the columns by James Wieghart of the *New York Daily News* Washington bureau are included in the figures for his paper (so as to reflect the production of the bureau), but are not credited to other papers that use his column.

4. The average number of Washington stories a day in the *Washington Post*, although highest of the twenty-two papers, is comparable to the averages of other papers. The only *Post* stories coded are those about national government that could just as well have been written by

Partly, of course, this reflects the fact all newspapers are hooked up to national services. Less than a third of Washington stories are staff-produced (29 percent); with the majority coming from the traditional wire services (57 percent)—Associated Press, United Press International, and, to a modest extent, Reuters; and the rest coming from the supplemental services (12 percent)—primarily the New York Times and the Los Angeles Times-Washington Post—and regional news services and free-lancers in Washington (2 percent).[5]

As far back as 1930, the editor of *Nation* noted how he read the same stories in the papers he bought at each train stop crossing the country.[6] Probably, in fact, the increased size and number of Washington bureaus of both independent newspapers and chains in recent years have decreased dependence on the wire services.[7] At the same time, the rise of the supplementals may be changing the type of stories that papers are taking from the wires.[8] A veteran Associated Press reporter contends, "Papers are increasingly using the supplementals for more of the big pieces and the wires for the 'cat and dog' stories."

---

reporters for other papers. No *Post* stories about local or social events are included, even though they have a Washington dateline.

5. Twenty-one of these papers belong to the Associated Press, seventeen subscribe to United Press International, and six to Reuters. One newspaper uses these sources for 88 percent of its Washington stories, four papers get over 75 percent of their Washington copy from the wires, while only one paper gets less than a fifth of its Washington reportage from AP and UPI. Of the twenty-two papers, nine receive copy from the Los Angeles Times-Washington Post news service, seven from the New York Times news service. Other supplementals represented: Dow Jones, Copley, Field, Newhouse, Knight-Ridder, Christian Science Monitor, Chicago Tribune-New York Daily News, and Congressional Quarterly. Sixteen of the papers use some material from regional news services or Washington free-lancers.

6. Oswald Garrison Villard, "The Press Today: V. Standardizing the Daily," *Nation*, June 4, 1930, p. 646.

7. There is a marked difference between independent and chain papers in the percentage of staff-written stories they publish. The chain-owned papers make much less use of their Washington bureaus. A reporter for one of the largest chains says that his operation is now exerting "subtle—and not so subtle—pressure on local editors to get them to make greater use of material" from their Washington bureau. He attributes low usage to the rapid growth of the chain. Many of their papers were recently acquired and "local editors are accustomed to, and comfortable with, [AP, UPI] wire copy." An editor of a paper just purchased by a chain hints that the paper asserts its "independence" by not using all the material from the new owner's Washington bureau.

8. Five papers in the sample use the supplementals for over 20 percent of their Washington stories. The *Greensburg Tribune-Review*, a western Pennsylvania newspaper without a Washington bureau, relies on a supplemental news service for one-third of its Washington stories. Furthermore, its supplemental service provides twice as many front-page Washington stories as the wire services.

A relatively constant number of Washington stories appear each day regardless of what goes on in the capital.[9] It does not make any difference, for example, that government offices are closed on weekends. Indeed, Sunday is a big day for running Washington stories. Half the papers sampled use more Washington stories on Sunday than on any other day. "My editors only want to know what I'm doing for Sunday," says a reporter for a major regional newspaper. Three papers run about twice as many Washington stories on Sunday as on weekdays, and at one paper the ratio is three to one. Clearly, this does not reflect a heavy news day; rather, the necessity is to fill an enlarged news hole created by heavy advertising.

So the quantity of Washington news that appears relates to availability (so much is being produced), to price (so much of it already has been paid for), to operational necessities (so much space must be filled), and to organizational maintenance (increased Washington staffs must have their material used).[10] Yet there must be other causes.

The dominance of Washington news cannot be explained solely in terms of media economics. Washington stories compete with those from other places. While perhaps not always so conveniently packaged as the Washington stories that flow in from the wire services, there is never a shortage of copy from other locations begging for attention. Editors tell us which stories they think are most important by where they place them. The stories judged to have the greatest impact, import, or interest become the front-page leads, usually at the top of the right-hand column on page 1, and here too Washington most often gets the place of honor:[11]

9. If all Washington stories were equally divided into seven parts, 14.3 percent would be printed each day, close to the actual distribution of Washington stories in the twenty-two papers. The variation is 3 percent or less for each day of the week except Monday (-6 percent).

10. Organizational maintenance also relates to the structure of news operations. For example, when Leon Sigal examined the stories that ran on page 1 of the *Washington Post* and the *New York Times* during 1970, he noted a pronounced tendency for each paper to display an equal number of items from the foreign, national, and metropolitan desks. This neat three-part arrangement hardly can be explained by some cosmic force that divides all happenings into three equal parts. See his *Reporters and Officials: The Organization and Politics of Newsmaking* (D. C. Heath, 1972), pp. 30–31.

11. The following is a tabulation of 153 editions of twenty-two newspapers. One paper does not publish on Sundays. For another, a tabloid with headlines and photographs—but no stories—on page 1, page 2 is coded as the front page. The impact of Washington reporters on front-page leads is actually somewhat greater than is shown by measuring datelines because two non-Washington stories were written by Washington reporters on assignment. Five of these papers are published in state capitals, so that some stories were coded under "state" although they also have a "local" dateline.

Dateline of story	Stories (percent)
Washington	45
Home state	19
Local	18
International	11
Another state	7

This is powerfully strange when it is recalled that the daily newspaper is the traditional fount of local news. As stated by Doris A. Graber, "[An] element in newsworthiness, which is particularly important for newspapers and local television, is that an event must be *close to home*. This heavy preference for local news rests on the assumption that people are most interested in what happens near them. Local media continue to exist because local events are their exclusive province, free from competition by national television and national print media."[12] But we find that nearly half of all newspapers' lead stories come from Washington; even more remarkable, all the top stories from the community, the state capital, and other cities in the home state combined do not equal the percentage from Washington.[13] Moreover, this is not a week in which great national events are luring editors away from local news.

These figures do not reflect an East Coast bias in favor of national government, which might be attributed to propinquity, for the newspaper with the most Washington news at the top of page 1 (six days out of seven) is in Seattle. The *Washington Post* (five days) is also a hometown paper for the capital; newspapers in San Diego, Los Angeles, Dallas, New Orleans, and Burlington, Vermont, follow with four days of Washington leads. In general, the newspapers in cities farthest from Washington most often view a Washington story as the top story of the day.

The sample is not biased in favor of papers noted for their national aspirations.[14] Papers from smaller cities are as interested in Washington

12. *Mass Media and American Politics* (Congressional Quarterly Press, 1980), p. 65. Italics in original.

13. See contra, Richard L. Rubin and Douglas Rivers, "The Mass Media and Critical Elections," paper delivered at the 1978 annual meeting of the Northeastern Political Science Association. The authors are in the process of doing "a systematic content analysis of six American newspapers from 1885 to 1975." When measuring "the three most prominent stories on the front page each day," they find content to be "heavily local in focus." However, they also note an "upward trend in national news." They conclude that "following 1932 the proportion of national political references increased relative to local political references."

14. See appendix table 23, for a list of the newspapers surveyed.

developments as those in major metropolitan areas: the *Anniston Star* and the *Chicago Tribune* print almost the same number of words from Washington. Nor does the rise in national news reflect the rise in chain-owned newspapers. The number of Washington stories do not correlate with type of ownership: one chain newspaper may run a lot of these stories, another only a few—being part of a group is not what makes the difference. (The sample, however, does not include any suburban dailies, which are becoming increasingly profitable by concentrating on local news.)

In Washington—as we previously speculated—the news has a rhythm set by newspaper reporters, notably of the inner ring, then travels a circuitous route back into the political government and out again to the rest of the country via the electronic media. It may be that the new accent of local papers on national news is part of this rhythm, as news on network television flows back into newspapers' communities and affects the consumers' expectations of what is important, hence newsworthy to local editors.

What stories are covered, at least from Washington, are decisions largely made by reporters; how prominently stories are played are decisions made in the home offices. Over seven days in April 1978, the editors of twenty-two newspapers chose twenty-eight different Washington events as the front-page leads, among them a proposal on Cyprus released by the Turkish Embassy, a report on solar energy from the President's Council on Environmental Quality, Senator Edward Kennedy "thinking" about running for president in 1980. Perhaps they were the most significant events in the world; more probably, editors—consciously or not—give extra weight to a Washington dateline.

WHAT is all this Washington news about?

We analyzed 1,878 newspaper stories and 132 television stories—a week's worth—to determine what institutions and subjects are covered. Up to three institutions and subjects were coded for each story. In an account of a trial in which the government was suing a corporation, for example, the institutions are judiciary, Justice Department, and private industry; the subjects are law and business.

There was also a head count of the people who appeared in print or on the air ("outputs"): senator (Democratic/Republican), House member (Democratic/Republican), civil servant, political appointee, and so on. Reporters, when filling out logs for a week, provided similar data about the people they interviewed ("inputs"). While it is unlovely to think of people as inputs and outputs, these terms permit easy comparison of what goes into the gathering of news and what comes out of the news gathering system.

The answers sought are not qualitative in the sense that these sums shed light on whether individual stories are fair or biased. Such efforts in the past have foundered on the shoals of definition. Yet in a broader sense, these are measurements of how evenhanded the press is in focusing on the various— and often competing—parts of the government process.

The answers, then, are to such questions as: Does the president receive more attention than the Congress? Does the Senate receive more attention than the House? Do majority and minority parties get the same notice? What stages of congressional action are covered? What types of congressional hearings are reported? What are the differences in the coverage of the different cabinet departments and the different subject areas?

The figures are presented separately for newspapers and network television. Regional news, however, is only of interest to newspapers.

A NOTABLE study of the attention paid by newspapers to the president and the Congress concludes that there has been "a long-term upward trend in overall Presidential news, both in absolute terms and relative to news about Congress."[15] This pattern, it is contended, gives the presidency "a distinct advantage in the struggle for political hegemony"[16] with "vast implications for the shaping both of national opinion and public policy."[17] Such conclusions tend to assume that it makes no difference whether the publicity is favorable or not.[18]

The Cornwell and Balutis studies examine front-page headlines and photographs from 1885 through 1974. But this being a book about Washington reporters, the focus is on the contents of the stories. The findings are different.

15. Elmer E. Cornwell, Jr., "Presidential News: The Expanding Public Image," *Journalism Quarterly*, vol. 36 (Summer 1959), p. 282. Cornwell examined two newspapers, the *New York Times* and the *Providence Journal*, from 1885 to 1957.

16. Alan P. Balutis, "The Presidency and the Press: The Expanding Presidential Image," *Presidential Studies Quarterly*, vol. 7 (Fall 1977), p. 251. Balutis carries forward Cornwell's research design from 1958 to 1974 using the *New York Times* and the *Buffalo Evening News*. He concludes that the gap grows wider between presidential and congressional news.

17. Elmer E. Cornwell, Jr., *Presidential Leadership of Public Opinion* (Indiana University Press, 1965), p. 4.

18. According to Roger H. Davidson and Glenn R. Parker, "perhaps it is not the content of the media messages, but simply the fact of extensive coverage, that elevates the standing of governmental institutions." See their "Positive Support for Political Institutions: The Case of Congress," *Western Political Quarterly*, vol. 25 (December 1972), p. 610.

Newspaper stories do not pay more attention to the president; television network stories do. It is true, of course, that there are short-term fluctuations. A colorful, activist president or an assertive Congress can expect to receive more press notice. In the period of this survey, 1978, most observers would say that, on the teeter-totter of politics, the Congress was up and the president down. However, since television and newspaper coverage were measured for the same days, the relative weight they gave to the White House and Capitol Hill is unaffected by these considerations. The following table shows the breakdown of the 921 newspaper stories and 87 network television stories about the president and the Congress:[19]

	Stories (percent)	
Subject of story	Newspaper	Television
President	46	59
Congress	54	41

Implicit in the earlier studies, strongly reaffirmed in this research, is that newspaper *headlines* favor the president. When the president or Congress appears in the headlines, 25 percent mention the president and 16 percent mention the Congress (as a percentage of all Washington stories). Furthermore, of the stories with neither the Congress nor the president in the headlines, many more are about the Congress (27 percent versus 10 percent). Counting headlines may be a legitimate measure of impact, but a highly misleading indicator of content.

Television as the medium of the presidency and the newspaper as the medium of the Congress are in keeping with the earlier computation of resource allocation by beat, showing a high percentage of Washington reporters (primarily working for newspapers) clustered on Capitol Hill. The three-ring-circus aspect of Congress, a body of 535 legislators, better fits the staff resources of newspapers; the unitary character of the presidency is easier for the television networks to cover. The president, an instantly recognizable figure, suits the needs of a visual medium; the regional character of Congress suits the localized needs of newspapers.

Whether one branch of government is advantaged by the media is an infinitely more complicated question than it may seem to be from adding up column inches or television seconds. An entirely different portrait of

19. Stories about both the president and the Congress are awarded to both institutions in our tabulations. Cornwell and Balutis exclude headlines about individual legislators, while this study includes such stories as congressional news.

Washington news emerges from counting the names of the persons that reporters interview than from counting the names that appear in newspapers or on television. When the sources that reporters say they go to for the stories they are working on are catalogued as legislative/political (members of Congress and their staffs) or executive/political (the president and all his appointees), 71 percent are legislative/political and 29 percent are executive/political. On the other hand, when the stories appear, a majority of the names are executive/political, 52 percent versus 48 percent.[20] "The best stories about the White House come from congressional sources," says a veteran reporter. This is a well-known "secret" in the press corps: *Washington news is funneled through Capitol Hill.*

This is not obvious to the newspaper reader or the television viewer or the researcher studying outputs, because reporters grant anonymity to congressional staffs. Many legislative aides, in the interest of good relations with their employers, prefer to keep their names out of the media. Reporters, at the same time, feel that identifying little-known assistants does not increase the value of their stories. It is the rare committee counsel, a John Doar ("Watergate") or a Leon Jaworski ("Koreagate"), whose name rates public notice. Of all those mentioned on the air or in print, only 1 percent are employees of Congress; of sixteen types of news sources identified (including civil service employees, officials of foreign governments, lobbyists, academics, and judges), congressional staff members rank fifteenth in frequency. Yet they account for 13 percent of all press contacts, the second largest category of reporters' informants. They are most often called upon when stories involve scandals, politics, foreign policy, and business—in that order. "Cultivate congressional staff members" is the advice given by a network correspondent specializing in economics.[21]

There are a variety of reasons that journalists prefer to gather information from the legislative branch. Most frequently mentioned is access—legislators and their aides are more willing to talk than executive-branch personnel. "On a scale of 100, Congress gets 95 percent for openness, downtown [the executive branch] gets less than 50 percent," says a reporter. It is more

20. These percentages represent 2,207 interviews by Washington reporters and names mentioned 4,184 times in their stories. Even if all civil servants are included in the executive-branch totals, the legislative branch is still more frequently interviewed, 36 percent versus 31 percent (as a percentage of all interviews).

21. While legislators and legislative staff are interviewed by reporters on many of the same topics (politics, lobbying, personalities, regional news), the survey shows that reporters more frequently talk with staff members than with legislators about such substantive topics as civil rights, business, social issues, and health.

difficult to reach a cabinet member than a senator, much more difficult to reach a subcabinet member than a senator's top aide. The people in the legislature view publicity as the lifeblood of elective politics; those in bureaus and agencies more often think of press attention as trouble. Reporters look for controversy, the enemy of efficient administration. Even White House aides note that having their names appear too often in the news may decrease their effectiveness in relations with colleagues.

Another reason reporters go to Capitol Hill for their stories is that they like the people who work there. "They're more like us." Bureaucrats, on the other hand, "don't talk English, they get wrapped up in technical terms." Moreover, the size and complexity of the executive branch make it difficult for generalist reporters to find their way through the maze of units and programs.[22]

Consider a hypothetical newspaper story. A reporter wants to check on a rumor that a certain water project is on the president's "hit list" and will not be included in the budget. Where should the reporter start his investigation? The Freedom of Information Act will not be of any help in getting documents in time for tomorrow's edition.

Who, then, should he call? The White House? The Office of Management and Budget? The Department of the Interior? If he calls a person too high in the hierarchy he is unlikely to be put through. If he calls a person too low in the bureaucracy he is apt to be referred to a public information office. If he calls a public information officer, he may be told that no final decision has been made—an exact truth, since there is no final decision until the president sends his message to Congress, yet possibly not the whole truth. Since the Interior Department is not the reporter's regular beat, he does not know any of the top people personally nor which executives are involved in this decision.

So the reporter's first two calls are to the legislator in whose district the water project is located and the staff director of the House (or Senate) Appropriations Subcommittee on Energy and Water Development. The member of Congress (or a personal assistant) has a vested interest in talking with the reporter; the staff director, though he does not know the reporter and

22. It may be, of course, that the degree to which reporters get their information from the legislative branch reflects the tremendous size of congressional staffs. The number of Senate and House committees and personal staff assistants numbered 13,763 in 1979, up from 2,129 in 1947. See Michael J. Malbin, *Unelected Representatives: Congressional Staff and the Future of Representational Government* (Basic Books, 1980), tables A-2 and A-5. However, since the expansion of a bureaucracy often makes information more difficult to get, it is probably the type of person they find there that accounts for reporters going to Capitol Hill.

has no special interest in the project, nevertheless has no reason not to talk with the reporter and may even consider the reporter a future source of favor and information. The reporter then writes a story about an executive-branch action—more than that, a presidential action—based on information from legislative-branch sources whose names are not likely to appear in the article.

Does it make any difference that a story about the executive branch comes from the legislative branch? Will the location of the sources affect the nature of the reportage? Yes, although the differences are hard to measure. Those who participate in government from the legislative and executive sides look at issues differently, they focus on different aspects of governance, and this will influence what they stress when talking with reporters.

On one level, such differences reflect the adversary relationship between executive and legislature. Even when both branches are controlled by the same political party, information gathered from Congress may accent the negative aspects of "downtown" decisions. The substantial growth in the congressional establishment increases the availability of material that casts the executive in an unfavorable light. But the outcomes of funneling Washington news through Capitol Hill can be more subtle: the natural interest of reporters in the politics of government—as opposed to the management of government—is reinforced by the similar interest of their legislative sources.[23] When journalists do interview civil servants, it is often on subjects that are given little press space: science and technology, civil rights, and health. On subjects such as energy, economics and finance, and regulatory policy, reporters seldom seek information from civil service employees. One experienced newsmagazine reporter notes with surprise, "The demographers at the Census Bureau are a gold mine." But the knowledge of those in the permanent government is, for most reporters, an untapped resource.

THE ATTENTION of the Washington press corps, as reflected in stories about Congress that appear in newspapers and on the television networks, is directed more to the Senate than to the House of Representatives.[24] This is moderately

23. The relative disinterest of Congress in executive-branch management may be changing somewhat in that the number of days of oversight hearings and meetings more than doubled in both House and Senate between the Ninety-first and Ninety-fourth Congresses. See Joel D. Aberbach, "Changes in Congressional Oversight," *American Behavioral Scientist*, vol. 22 (May–June 1979), p. 507.

24. The gap between Senate and House coverage may be greater than usual during the week under study because the major congressional event was consideration of a treaty, an exclusive constitutional concern of the Senate. This would particularly inflate the Senate percentage of TV coverage since television always focuses on the "big story."

the case for newspapers, 54 percent versus 46 percent, but is overwhelmingly true of television network coverage, where the breakdown of Senate and House stories is two-thirds and one-third, 66 percent about the Senate and 34 percent about the House.[25]

Regional news, an important part of newspapers' mandate, tends to center in the House; the smaller Senate is easier for television to cover; cameras are attracted to well-recognized faces, celebrities who become known through national campaigns or activities that predate their senatorial service (during this period: Edward Kennedy, Daniel Patrick Moynihan, S. I. Hayakawa, George McGovern, Barry Goldwater, Charles Percy, John Glenn, Robert Dole, Edmund Muskie, Howard Baker, Henry Jackson).

To test the proposition that senators—rather than the Senate per se—make television news, the survey counts the number of times that legislators' names appear in news stories. In newspapers, senators receive only 5 percent more attention than House members; but on the television network evening news programs, 73 percent of the legislators mentioned are senators. Clearly, most House members lack the glitter that attracts a visual medium. Television, if it had been around in 1831, would have noticed Congressman John Quincy Adams, but only because he was an ex-president; in 1848, it would not have noticed Congressman Abraham Lincoln.

In newspaper stories, senators overwhelmingly dominate in the area of foreign policy (only 14 percent of the lawmakers referred to are in the House), but members of the House are more often cited in stories about economics and finance (60 percent to 40 percent). This reflects the special roles that the Constitution gives to the Senate in foreign policy and to the House in originating revenue bills. In these cases, maintaining numerical balances would be its own form of distortion.

The composition of the House of Representatives during this period was 63.5 percent Democratic and 36.5 percent Republican. Of House members mentioned in news stories, 76 percent are Democratic and 24 percent Republican. Relative to their numerical strength, House Republicans receive 12 percent fewer references than their colleagues across the aisle.

The Senate consisted of fifty-nine Democrats and forty-one Republicans;[26]

25. The data on House and Senate coverage were computed in two ways: one coded all references to legislators; the other coded only instances where legislators are quoted or interviewed. The gap in television coverage between House and Senate narrows slightly (less than 5 percent) when all references are included, indicating that House members receive somewhat more incidental notice than senators, tending to be mentioned rather than quoted.

26. For the purposes of this study, Senator Harry F. Byrd, Jr., of Virginia, Independent, is counted with the Democrats because he receives his committee assignments through the Democratic Caucus.

the Democrats receive 69 percent of the news media's attention. Senate Republicans, at 31 percent, do slightly better than House Republicans. The big difference in coverage by party is in television, where House Republicans are 27 percent behind House Democrats, and Republican senators trail Democratic senators by 17 percent.

When the figures for the House and Senate are combined, the Democrats get attention that exceeds the party's numerical advantage by 10 percent. Some will contend that this is evidence of a Democratic leaning in the Washington news corps. Others could argue that 10 percent represents a press "bonus" to the majority party. Whenever a committee chairman is quoted, for example, that person has to be a Democrat. "Reporters don't care what the Republicans say simply because they're not in control," says a young Washington reporter. With Republicans taking control in 1981, the proposition should be tested.

Republican members of the House of Representatives are doubly disadvantaged, being from the House and being from the minority party. Much of this underrepresentation comes in television: the evening news programs of the three television networks during a five-day period only twice mention Republican House members.

On newspaper stories about politics, the tabulation by party of House members shows that 64 percent of those named are Democrats, 36 percent are Republicans—less than 1 percent different from the numerical party balance. The following table shows the percentages for Democratic and Republican senators mentioned in a selected number of subject areas, including politics:

	Party of senator named in story (percent)	
Subject of story	Democrat	Republican
Energy	83.6	16.4
Foreign policy	77.3	22.7
Economics	77.2	22.8
Politics	49.5	50.5

Evidently reporters interview an equal number of Republicans and Democrats only when their stories are about politics.

Assuming that balance is something reporters strive for, these data suggest how far they fall short of their goal. Of course, we have been measuring a large number of factors: executive/legislative, House/Senate, congressional Democrats/congressional Republicans, House Democrats/House Republicans, Senate Democrats/Senate Republicans. For the individual reporter, keeping all of these in balance within each story would be like playing three-dimensional chess.

Yet certain balances are more important to reporters than others. They deliberately seek balance on stories that involve "scandal." When a congressional committee or an individual legislator, for example, makes charges against someone or some agency in the executive branch, that person or agency is asked to respond.[27] In substantive areas, however, there are extreme differences in the number of Democrats and Republicans mentioned. Since all Democrats are not on one side of an issue and all Republicans on the other, this is not proof that reporters fail to pay the same attention to both sides of a question, only that they fail to give equal space to both political parties, except on stories about politics.

Do NEWSPAPERS and network television accurately reflect the relative importance of the different stages in the legislative process? How much weight is given to crucial work in committees? Or do the media simply focus on the drama of a final vote in the Senate or House of Representatives? If the press is to notify citizens of pending actions in sufficient time for them to make their views known to their representatives it would have to devote a substantial portion of congressional coverage to the early stages of legislative development, especially during that part of the year when the committees are most active.[28]

	Stories (percent)	
Legislative stage in story	Newspapers	Television
Introduction of legislation	3	0
Subcommittees	20	7
Committees	37	24
Floor action	35	58
Conference committees	5	11

Television attention appears to gain momentum as a bill moves along the legislative route, reaching a crescendo when a final action is taken. A long-

27. On stories coded as "scandals," the balancing of conflicting positions is reflected in a 53:47 division between legislative and executive personnel mentioned. There is a similar finding in David L. Paletz, "Media Coverage of Interest Groups in the U.S.A.: An Initial Case Study," a paper prepared for the 11th Congress, International Association for Mass Communication Research, Warsaw, Poland, September 4–9, 1978.

28. March and April are the busiest months for committee and subcommittee meetings; in 1975, 13 percent of all Senate meetings were held in each of these months. See *Legislative Activity Sourcebook: United States Senate*, prepared for the Commission on the Operation of the Senate, 94 Cong. 2 sess. (Government Printing Office, 1976), p. 6.

term study would show that this is not a fixed pattern. For example, when Robinson and Appel examined five weeks of television network news in January and February 1976, 14 percent of the stories involved floor action and 35 percent committee action. The period they studied was earlier in the congressional session than the one analyzed here and included a House committee investigation of CIA abuses in Chile.[29] Television simply goes after the top congressional story, regardless of where it occurs in the legislative process. In the April 1978 period its concentration was on four events: the floor debate on the Panama Canal treaties, a vote in the House of Representatives on the Emergency Farm Bill, a vote by the House Ways and Means Committee on tuition tax credits, and a conference committee attempt to reach agreement on an energy bill. Viewers are given highlights within a half-hour format, rather than the full panoply of issues, interests, and participants that converge daily on Capitol Hill. If this is their only source of information, television viewers might wonder where the parts fit into the whole.

Newspapers, too, focus on the top stories—the same ones the television networks focus on—but they have the staff resources, the available space, and the mission (in the case of regional news) to pay attention to other activities as well. Their distribution of stories by legislative stages mirrors the textbook definition of where the "real" work of Congress takes place. These data do not imply that newspaper coverage is less episodic than television, only that it is spaced more evenly along the legislative spectrum. Still, with over half of their legislative stories on subcommittee and committee activities, newspapers might be said to provide an "early warning system."

During the week in April 1978 there were 179 congressional committee or subcommittee sessions that heard witnesses and were open to the press.[30] The twenty-two newspapers contained stories about 38 hearings, or 21 percent of what was available. Although not all stories appeared in every paper, the repetition of certain stories indicates that all the hearings the press considers

29. See Michael J. Robinson and Kevin R. Appel, "Network News Coverage of Congress," *Political Science Quarterly*, vol. 94 (Fall 1979), pp. 410–11. The authors believe that TV's accent on committee action in their 1976 study reflects the fact that cameras were allowed into the committee rooms but not onto the House floor. Clearly this was not a major factor in this 1978 survey. In 1979, House taping of floor action was made available to TV; filming is still not permitted on the Senate floor. It would be interesting to see to what extent the availability of moving pictures has increased network TV coverage of House floor deliberations.

30. There were also twenty closed hearings and forty-five congressional committee meetings that were not hearings. This analysis compares newspaper stories with the summaries of congressional committee activities that are given in the "Daily Digest" at the end of each day's *Congressional Record*.

important are included in the sample. This does not mean, of course, that 79 percent of the hearings go unreported: other hearings are of regional interest to other papers. Also, many hearings are on subjects without mass appeal (a proposed budget to administer the Trust Territory of the Pacific Islands or the appropriations for the Marine Mammal Commission, for example). Still, 21 percent may seem a modest figure.

Members of Congress complain about the lack of news attention. But should any news corps be expected to cover 179 congressional hearings during a five-day period? The small percentage of hearings that gets reported might be viewed as an indictment of the proliferation of congressional committees, particularly in the House of Representatives, where the number of standing committees and subcommittees has reached 168. Are there too few reporters or too many hearings? If Congress wishes adequate press coverage, it needs to worry about whether committee activities have surpassed the resources that can be marshaled by news organizations.

Of the 179 open hearings, 110 were in the House of Representatives, 67 were in the Senate, 2 were in joint committees. There were newspaper stories on 16 percent (18) of the House sessions, and 28 percent (19) of the Senate's, producing sixty stories about the House hearings and fifty-nine about those in the Senate.

If House members are the overlooked legislators, the same cannot be said of House committee hearings. It might appear that equal coverage is achieved by the House working nearly twice as hard as the Senate, but it is doubtful that House committee coverage would be cut in half if its sessions were halved. Large bureaus usually assign a reporter to each chamber and, except for regional news, equal coverage of House and Senate hearings reflects equal allocation of press resources. House committees may compete against each other for reporters' attention, as do Senate committees.

Nearly a third of the hearings are covered because something being discussed is about the reporter's circulation area or because people from his circulation area are testifying. Over a fourth are hearings with "star" witnesses; advance notice that a committee will be listening to Edward Kennedy, Ralph Nader, the chairman of the Federal Reserve Board, the director of the FBI, or a cabinet officer is a sure predictor that a story will be in the next day's paper. In some instances, this is simply a case of "names make news." But people in important positions also often make important news. "Scandals" are the topics of 8 percent of the hearings covered (21 percent of the published stories that emanated from congressional hearings are about scandals). So two-thirds of committee coverage can be attributed to regional news or stars or scandal.

The other third of the hearings can be considered "discretionary," hearings that reporters go to solely because they think they will be interesting or important. Some journalists are critical of their colleagues on this score. Says one newspaper reporter, "I was practically alone at these population hearings because such stuff isn't fashionable to Washington reporters."

ALL CABINET departments are equal, but some are more equal than others, to paraphrase George Orwell. Differences are implicit in Thomas E. Cronin's useful distinction between an inner cabinet and an outer cabinet.[31] The inner cabinet is the departments of State, Defense, Treasury, and Justice. All others are in the outer cabinet. The press, especially network television, is attracted to the inner cabinet, which tends to cast the outer cabinet into even greater darkness.

Of the newspaper stories from Washington during the week surveyed, 12 percent involve the inner cabinet and 9 percent involve the outer cabinet. On the network television evening news programs, stories of the inner cabinet amount to 19 percent of the total, those of the outer cabinet are 4 percent of the total.

The percentage of attention paid to each department changes from week to week, of course. For example, during the five days of television news studied, there was an Agriculture Department story but no Labor Department story (an important farm bill was being voted on in Congress); in some future week there will be a Labor story, but, one suspects, it will replace an Agriculture story, not a State Department story. The ratio of news about the inner cabinet and outer cabinet probably remains fairly constant; over time, however, government creates more and more agencies that contend for the outer cabinet's share of the news hole.[32]

The inner cabinet has been around since George Washington was president. Its activities always will form the core of executive agency news. On the other hand, the outer cabinet is composed of successive waves of important groups that have been able to win departmental status for their interests (Labor, Agriculture, Commerce, Education) and domestic concerns that have risen in national importance (Interior, Health and Human Services, Housing and Urban Development, Transportation, Energy). These agencies compete for the news space that is left after notice has been taken of the

31. See *The State of the Presidency* (Little, Brown, 1975), pp. 188–92. Cronin's inner and outer cabinets are meant to indicate "how White House aides view the departments."

32. The disparity in newspaper attention to inner and outer cabinets narrows if non-Washington stories generated by federal regional offices are counted, for these offices are primarily branches of outer-cabinet departments.

president, the Congress, the inner cabinet, and the Supreme Court. Eventually the proliferation of government agencies—just as of congressional committees—may outstrip the resources of the media.

Press coverage of the executive branch is also made more difficult by geographical dispersion, as the Pentagon and such agencies as the Bureau of the Census, the National Bureau of Standards, the National Institutes of Health, the Food and Drug Administration, and the Social Security Administration are located in Maryland and Virginia. At least the work of Congress is clustered around Capitol Hill.

How government draws the boxes on its organization chart and where it places the buildings become factors in how the press covers government, although it is doubtful that government designers take this into account. Fewer departments, for example—such as Richard Nixon proposed in 1971[33]—would result in more evenly distributed press coverage.

NEWSPAPERS and television have roughly the same priorities in the subjects of their Washington stories. Eleven subjects account for 66 percent of the newspapers' Washington stories and 81 percent of television news stories. Of the eleven subjects, nine appear on both lists. Thirty subjects receive some attention in newspapers' Washington stories. Television covers fewer subjects (twenty-four) but gives the top ones more attention, which has the effect of making television's emphasis on foreign policy twice that of newspapers.[34]

The subjects are primarily determined by newsmakers themselves. Even the 6 percent of the news hole devoted to scandals mainly reflects congressional investigations rather than the initiatives of news organizations.[35] When the Senate is debating the Panama Canal treaties and the U.S. president is

33. In this message to Congress, March 25, 1971, President Nixon proposed retaining the departments of State, Treasury, Defense, and Justice, and replacing the other seven departments with four new departments: Natural Resources, Human Resources, Economic Affairs, and Community Development. See *Papers Relating to the President's Departmental Reorganization Program: A Reference Compilation* (GPO, March 1971), p. 25.

34. The State Department is the source of 6 percent of television stories, 3 percent of newspaper stories. Newspapers, on the other hand, concentrate more on nongovernmental entities in Washington, such as industry, labor unions, trade associations, and lobbies (19 percent for newspapers and 11 percent for television).

35. The newspapers surveyed give considerably different play to scandals, ranging from 1 to 8 percent of their Washington news hole. Thirteen papers run scandals on page 1, nine do not. Chain-owned papers are less likely to devote as much space to scandals as the independents. Whether papers have direct, indirect, or no competition is not a clue to the attention paid. Placement and the number of such stories are not related to the political coloration of the papers' editorial policies. Perhaps all that can be concluded is that certain papers have a muckraking tradition without regard to other variables. The *New York Daily News* and the *Washington Post*, for example, ranked first and second in stories about scandals.

meeting with the Rumanian president and the secretary of state is touring
Africa, they must be reported; and they are news about foreign policy. But
what also contributes to the dominance of foreign policy news is that it
interests reporters. Those who can cover any subject—class A general
assignment reporters—overwhelmingly choose to write about politics and
foreign policy. They do so despite their belief that public interest in
international news is low.[36] Thus foreign policy ranks first in coverage by
both newspapers and television. The following tables summarize the data:

Washington stories, newspapers

Subject	Rank	Percent
Foreign policy	1	12.0
Economics/finance	2	10.9
Government operations	3	6.7
Scandals	4	6.4
Law	5	5.9
Politics	6	4.7
Business	7	4.7
Energy	8	4.3
Agriculture	9	3.8
Defense	10/11	3.3
Regulatory policy	10/11	3.3

Washington stories, television

Subject	Rank	Percent
Foreign policy	1	24.0
Economics/finance	2	17.0
Scandals	3	6.0
Politics	4/5	5.5
Agriculture	4/5	5.5
Law	6	5.0
Consumer affairs	7	4.5
Energy	8/9	3.5
Defense	8/9	3.5
Government operations	10/11	3.0
Education	10/11	3.0

Nearly a third of the Washington newspaper stories on the front pages deal
with foreign policy and economics/finance.[37] These are also areas that rank

36. See Stanley Foundation, *Strategy for Peace: U.S. Foreign Policy Conference, October
25–28, 1979* (Muscatine, Iowa: Stanley Foundation, 1980), p. 56.

37. A tabulation of the subjects that radio and wire service reporters write about also shows
foreign policy and economics/finance in first and second places. The combined figures are 23
percent for the wires and 33 percent for radio. The ranking of subjects for radio reporters closely
approximates that of television.

high in the number of interpretive stories.[38] Reporters assigned to the State Department write about foreign policy and reporters at Treasury write about economics/finance, but so too do reporters on virtually every beat whether or not they have any special training or experience in these areas. Despite the increased specialization of the press corps, the nature of general circulation journalism is that most stories—when viewed by subject content—are written by nonexperts. The White House beat illustrates the range of news topics at a key location during a week:[39]

Stories by White House reporters

Subject	Rank	Percent
Foreign policy	1	26.6
Politics	2	21.5
Personalities	3	12.7
Economics/finance	4	8.0
Government operations	5	6.8
Defense	6	5.1
Energy	7	3.0
Regional	8	2.5

Foreign policy, economics/finance, and politics weave in and out of the news that originates in the capital. On seven of thirteen major beats, more than 9 percent of the output is about politics. Reporters consider themselves experts on politics and would like to be experts on foreign policy. What of economics/finance? It is a subject that many of them wish would go away. As we have seen, the economics beat ranks eleventh in prestige. But it cannot be ignored, even though it can sometimes be assigned to the junior members of the bureau. Those on class B general assignments, usually the youngest and most inexperienced reporters, devote more attention to economics/finance than to any other subject. In 1978, the Washington press corps was strangely out of tune—in personal interest, at least—with an area that was increasingly the subject of the events that had to be covered.

38. Newspaper articles that are meant to be interpretations of events fill 8 percent of the Washington news hole, but constitute 11 percent of the stories about foreign policy, 11 percent of government operations stories, and 9 percent of economics/finance stories. This compares, for example, with 3 percent for law. In three-quarters of the stories the readers are clearly told that they are being given "analysis" or "commentary."

39. Subjects that receive at least 2 percent of White House reporters' attention are included; the other stories (13.8 percent) cover fifteen additional subjects, including health, labor, agriculture, and education.

NETWORK television need not be concerned about local angles, but every daily newspaper with a Washington bureau (except those specializing in business) considers covering regional news as one of its purposes. A *New York Times* reporter says, "We're producing a national product. There's one guy here who writes for the metro desk [in New York]. This used to give the others an excuse for not having to worry about the regional angle. But this is changing a bit. The change is subtle, not radical. The editors in New York are continually pressing for it. So now many stories have 'regional impact' in the fifth or sixth paragraph."

Regional news, as used here, is a story specifically about a person in Washington from the "home town" or about a federal government action that affects the paper's circulation area. The following is from the *Milwaukee Journal*, April 11, 1978:

REUSS STRIVES FOR 'MIRACLE' TO GET FEDERAL BUILDING
By John W. Kole, Journal Washington Bureau

WASHINGTON, D.C.—Hoping to overcome the negative attitude of President Carter's budget office, Rep. Henry S. Reuss (D–Wis.) said Tuesday that while he believed it would take a miracle to salvage Milwaukee's proposed new federal building . . . .

Regional angle news is a national story that mentions a local person or place. From the *Des Moines Register*, April 10, 1978:

WATERLOO-BORN ASSASSINATION SUSPECT HELD

WASHINGTON, D.C. (AP)—Michael Vernon Townley, 35, wanted for questioning in the 1976 assassination of former Chilean diplomat Orlando Letelier, was taken into custody Sunday by the FBI after a flight from Chile.

FBI spokesman Tom Harrington said Townley, born in Waterloo, Ia., was being held at Fort Meade, . . .

A more typical regional angle would be an account of the defeat of the emergency farm bill in the House of Representatives, a national story, in which the vote of the district's representative is given.

Fifteen percent of Washington stories contain some regional angle.[40] The range for individual newspapers is 27 percent to 3 percent. (The *Washington Post* was not computed.) Five newspapers rate above 20 percent. Seven papers are below 10 percent. No special geographic patterns emerge; for example, the highest and lowest percentages are from papers in comparable eastern

---

40. The president, vice president, and high appointed officials are not included in the coding of regional stories. Congress is included, however, and a newspaper will be high on the regional-angle scale without really trying if it is located in a state whose congressional delegation includes nationally prominent legislators. Yet the scale does prove sensitive to variations in the efforts of the different newspapers to relate Washington to their communities.

cities. The three papers of smallest circulation, however, are clustered near the bottom of the list.[41]

Regional news, the specially crafted story about Washington from a local perspective, is a very much smaller part of the Washington news hole (less than 2 percent of the subjects coded). Because regional news is designed for one outlet, each story is counted once, while each wire service story appears in papers across the country. Still, if it is not unreasonable to assume that a newspaper should devote at least 1 percent of its Washington coverage to stories of special interest to its community, then nearly half of these papers flunk this test (ten of twenty-one). Five papers run no regional news at all.

The traditional wire services are now out of the business of producing regional news. The regional news services in Washington operate at bare subsistence levels. Reporters for local television stations do a great deal of regional news, but few stations have their own reporters in Washington.[42] Local newspaper editors complain a lot about the Washington bureaus' failures to relate the news to their locales, but rarely do they put stories from their regional reporters in Washington on the front page. Washington regional reporters rarely earn as much as Washington national reporters. Of the thirteen beats ranked by prestige, regional news ranks thirteenth.

What these data suggest is a drift from regional news reporting to regional-angle reporting, as reporters do what they really want to do (cover national and international events) and pay their dues to their communities with passing references. Increasingly, the contents of the news from Washington in papers around the country look more and more like the *New York Times*.

41. Regional angles can be added to Washington stories by home-office editors. Regional news must be written in Washington. This may be one reason that chain-owned newspapers are substantially behind the independents in number of regional-angle stories published, even though their Washington bureaus do well in producing regional news stories.

42. Reporters covering Washington for television stations spend 19 percent of their time on regional news.

CHAPTER SIX

Impressions

WASHINGTON is more and more the center of attention in the nation's news media, dominating even when nothing very special happens in the capital. There are consequences for public policy when the information that citizens receive is overwhelmingly about one level of government.

The television networks and the weekly newsmagazines must be national in character, of course, yet a conclusion of this study is that so too are newspapers, to a surprising degree.

News comes from where reporters are: the increase in Washington stories reflects growth in the Washington press corps.[1] This growth in personnel, argues a reporter for Knight-Ridder, "is a miracle in that Washington coverage drains, rather than produces, revenue." While true, most newspapers get most of their Washington stories from the wire services and, increasingly, from the supplemental news services, where the costs to local papers are constant regardless of the amount used. In comparison with state and local stories, which are more apt to be staff-produced, Washington stories are a bargain. Thus the increase in Washington stories is a product both of newspapers' willingness to spend money on coverage that they think is important and prestigious and of a system that provides them with plentiful and inexpensive copy.

Given the limits to the size of newspapers' news holes, a rise in Washington stories presages a decline in news of municipal and state governments, most often the latter. David Morgan's examination of political news in eleven New York state newspapers supports this prediction.[2] The average percentages are: local, 18; state, 21; *national*, 42; and international, 19. Excluding the two Albany newspapers from the tabulation, only 16 percent of political news is of the state. The *least* Washington news carried by any of the nine papers

1. For more on this phenomenon ("news is where you look for it"), see Michael A. DuBick, "The Organizational Structure of Newspapers in Relation to their Metropolitan Environments," *Administrative Science Quarterly*, vol. 23 (September 1978), p. 419.

2. *The Capital Press Corps: Newsmen and the Governing of New York State* (Greenwood Press, 1978), table 2.4.

outside of Albany is 31 percent of its total political news, greater than the *most* local news (27 percent) or state news (22 percent) any of them carry. An irony of the modest space devoted to state news is that the public learns little about the increasing number of federal programs administered by state governments. Unfortunately, the relationship between the press and federalism is a subject with few students.

Despite reliance on prepaid Washington stories—and because so many stories are available—American newspapers have not turned into clones. Editors do select Washington stories that reflect the economic and demographic interests of their communities. Of the twenty-two papers in the survey, the *Des Moines Register* is first in agriculture stories, the *Seattle Times* is first in the conservation/environment category; the *Times-Picayune*, in the port city of New Orleans, is first in transportation; the large black population of Baltimore may account for the *News American* being first in civil rights stories.[3] Group ownership of newspapers, although it might seem a force for standardization, has not had this effect on the news produced by chain bureaus in Washington, which focus more on regional stories than the independents do. Some papers that have become part of a chain have Washington reporting about their regions for the first time.

THE SHEER volume of words that flows from Washington is remarkable; there has never been a place so extensively covered on a permanent basis. Yet Washington reporters currently feel themselves under attack. Of course, an individual reader is exposed to only a small percentage of the news available, so from whose perspective should the adequacy of Washington news be judged? Those who need only know the outlines of what happens each day are well served by mass journalism, which, like fast-food chains, can quickly and inexpensively produce quantities of a bland diet. And most readers with professional or occupational needs for detailed information about specialized subjects are also well served; a notable development of recent years is the

3. Perhaps the legendary love of politics that is attributed to Texans is borne out by the fact that no paper in the survey devotes a larger percentage of its Washington stories to politics than the *Dallas Morning News*. There are other reasons for special emphasis, of course. The *Los Angeles Times* runs three times the average percentage of stories about social issues—such as trends in the aging or youth populations—undoubtedly reflecting an editorial decision on the nature of the product. The large percentage of stories on appointments and nominations in the *Pittsburgh Press*, on the other hand, merely mirrors the events of a week in which a number of Pennsylvanians were appointed to office or involved in nomination controversies. But in some cases it is difficult to ascertain the reasons for special emphasis. Why, for example, does the *Denver Post* rank first in stories about the postal service?

extent to which news is tailored to limited audiences. Any group of a thousand buyers, it is said, who can pass along the high subscription cost to employers or the government (through income tax deductions), eventually become the target of a Washington reporting operation.

Somewhere in between these extremes there are aggrieved consumers. Perhaps they should not expect total satisfaction for the price of a newspaper or a television set. These media by design cater to a broad variety of tastes and interests. Americans, however, have never been agreeable to lowering their expectations or keeping their complaints to themselves.

Among the criticisms of the press is that it slants the news, an accusation often coming from the right and the left at the same time. This study does not measure news content against some objective version of reality, but does throw light on the politics of Washington reporters. Slightly more than half of the reporters believe the news corps has a political bias, which they overwhelmingly think is liberal. Yet they often rate themselves more conservative than this image. There is also evidence that reporters working for the influential news organizations judge the press corps to be more liberal than do other reporters. In general, however, this study concludes that Washington reporters are more apolitical than press critics contend. The slant of Washington news is more a product of the angle from which it is observed than from ideology.

Most reporters attempt to quantify fairness by awarding equal space or equal time. But the growing bigness and complexity of the federal establishment make this increasingly difficult. In a complicated and pluralistic society it is hard to know what interests to balance. We find that reporters apply their fairness doctrine very narrowly—to stories with two clear sides, Republican and Democrat, attacker and attacked.[4] Our measurements fail to pick up balances in stories other than politics and scandals, suggesting that reporters may ignore or deny the problem or don't know who all the actors are.

In addition to the professional and personal standards of reporters conventions of what is news and restrictions of the law and marketplace govern what reporters write. A national political correspondent learns troubling things about the temperament of a presidential candidate from the way he plays poker. He does not write this for his newspaper. Playing poker on a campaign plane is not news.[5] Measured against the sum of everything that

---

4. For a comment on newspaper coverage of scandals see chapter 5, note 35.

5. See Lou Cannon, *Reporting: An Inside View* (California Journal Press, 1977), pp. 157–58.

happens (even to famous people), the band of happenings the media records is narrow.

Some influences on public affairs, such as individual psychology and group dynamics, cannot be fitted into the conventional objective news style. Interpretive reporting may then be employed to go "behind the news." Interpretation, though a small percentage of Washington stories, is expanding. No conspiracy theories apply; interpretation is not advocacy. Still, it is one step removed from value-free standards. Objectivity in journalism is a much-abused concept. It can be no more than an ideal and a flawed representation of reality. But it is also an internal check on the power of the press. The trend away from the objective news style comes at a time when at least one serious student argues that the press has turned into "perhaps the second most powerful institution in the country next to the presidency."[6]

"ONE'S impression," wrote Daniel Patrick Moynihan in 1971, "is that twenty years and more ago the preponderance of the 'working press' (as it liked to call itself) was surprisingly close in origins and attitudes to working people generally. They were not Ivy Leaguers. They now are or soon will be. Journalism has become, if not an elite profession, a profession attracted to elites. This is noticeably so in Washington."[7] Moynihan understands the historical class origins of journalism. Max Weber said in 1918 that "the journalist belongs to a sort of pariah caste."[8] Yet Rosten's study of 1936 and Rivers's of 1951 show the degree to which Washington reporters had already moved up in social standing.[9] Having 80 percent of reporters with at least some college education in or before the Great Depression suggests a rather steep departure from pariah status.

Some reporters challenge Moynihan's categorization of the Washington press as Ivy Leaguers. But surely he speaks symbolically, given the impressionistic nature of the essay. He might have said, "Nearly 35 percent of the Washington press corps attended colleges or universities rated as highly selective, a category that includes, in addition to the Ivy League, such other

6. See Max M. Kampelman, "The Power of the Press: A Problem for Our Democracy," *Policy Review*, no. 6 (Fall 1978), p. 7.

7. "The Presidency and the Press," in Moynihan, *Coping: Essays on the Practice of Government* (Random House, 1973), p. 319. First published in *Commentary*, vol. 51 (March 1971), pp. 41–52.

8. From Jeremy Tunstall, *Journalists at Work* (Sage, 1971), p. 9.

9. Leo C. Rosten, *The Washington Correspondents* (1937; reprint ed., Arno Press, 1974); William L. Rivers, "The Correspondents after 25 Years," *Columbia Journalism Review*, vol. 1 (Spring 1962).

institutions as Amherst, Brandeis, Bryn Mawr, Carleton, the University of Chicago, Haverford, Johns Hopkins, Massachusetts Institute of Technology, Mount Holyoke, Oberlin, Reed, Rice, Smith, Stanford, Swarthmore, Wellesley, Wesleyan, and Williams." Then he would be correct, exactly, though the sentence is not as felicitous.

Being described as an elite disturbs many reporters. But, of course, they are. And those who eventually join their ranks—regardless of race, religion, gender, or previous economic condition—also will be part of this elite. They are workers in words and symbols. They must be trained in the skills necessary for the occupation, meaning that they will be increasingly well schooled. They will be increasingly well compensated. They will be increasingly fraternal with those of comparable standing.

The news business has not been an equal opportunity employer. Changes are taking place, but the rate of change is slow, at least in Washington. In terms of demographics, if there is an average Washington reporter and an average American, they do not look much like each other. The influential Washington reporter looks even less like the average American. Does this make a difference in how the news is reported? In some instances the answer is yes. It would be healthier in a democratic society for reporters for the general circulation press to try to narrow the distinctions that separate them from their customers. A reporter writes a perceptive article about how the small-town backgrounds of President Carter's top aides affect White House decisionmaking, drawing on his own experiences growing up in a town with a population of 2,000.[10] Perhaps the same writer could have brought equal insight to an explanation of President Kennedy's inner circle of northern urban Irish Catholics, but his life has not prepared him to make the connections. Demographic characteristics of the work force do have an effect on the finished product. Producing news is not like the production of iron and steel.

However, the more basic consideration—more basic because it ultimately affects all reporters regardless of their backgrounds—is the inherent separation between Washington and the rest of the nation. (It is a problem also for government officials, as reporters are quick to note.) The reporters' Washington is not a city of dentists, insurance agents, Rotary, and Little League. It is not New York, Chicago, or Los Angeles scaled down. It is more like Albany, Springfield, or Sacramento writ large. The world of Washington reporters is inhabited by legislators and their staffs, political executives, bureaucrats,

10. See Dennis Farney, "Lance and the Small-Town Boys," *Wall Street Journal*, September 23, 1977.

diplomats, lobbyists, and, above all, by other reporters. The echo chamber of this world gives a special resonance, like the corridors in a hospital or penal institution. The sound on the inside is different from the outside; not right or wrong, simply different. Creating a one-industry capital can cause problems.

A press corps that reflects the population casts its net of interests wider. But female reporters in Washington, for example, are no more likely to interview "the average woman" than male Washington reporters focus on "the man in the street." They are in Washington to cover established institutions, almost exclusively governmental or allied to government. They report on elites, a term as offensive to the subjects of their attention as it is to them. Washington news gathering, in other words, is an interaction among elites. One elite reports on another elite.[11] This is not meant to be a pejorative statement.

YET SOME reporters will be offended, in which case they will have to redefine news, as those on the political left attempted to do in the 1960s under such rubrics as alternative journalism, new journalism, advocacy journalism. The new journalism used fictive forms instead of the conventional journalistic style of who-what-where-when-how. It tried to provide an alternative to news from the "establishment." It advanced a point of view, arguing that there can be no objectivity, that facts are disputable and carefully selected (or excluded) anyway. The new journalism was aimed primarily at young people, whose interests determined the subject matter.[12]

A Washington version of redefined news might be called social science journalism. Its roots are not in the youth movement of the 1960s (which has little effect on the Washington press corps, especially young reporters) but in the discontent of the intelligentsia. Most of its strongest advocates are older reporters. The literary model is not fiction but the social sciences, and it focuses on government problems rather than life styles. Its style of writing owes more to the *Wall Street Journal* than the *Berkeley Barb*, the accent on greater interpretation results more from the internal dynamics of the *Washington Post* than *Rolling Stone*.

The redefinition of news is in response to criticism from journalists associated with inner-ring newspapers. "We [the press] are fascinated by

11. See Herbert J. Gans, *Deciding What's News: A Study of CBS Evening News, NBC Nightly News, Newsweek, and Time* (Pantheon, 1979), p. 61.

12. See Everette E. Dennis and William L. Rivers, *Other Voices: The New Journalism in America* (San Francisco: Canfield Press, 1974), especially chap. 1.

events but not by the things that *cause* the events," writes James Reston, *New York Times* columnist and former Washington bureau chief.[13] Writes Philip Foisie, an editor of the *Washington Post*, "We [the press] have not developed the knack of identifying and writing regularly about problems *before* they become crises."[14] Their views are widely held, as illustrated by the conclusions of two surveys of Washington reporters calling for "more substantive journalism" and the exploration of "important but undercovered areas of the news."[15] Social science journalism, then, can be defined as serious, dealing with cause, and predictive (before the crisis). Conversely, it deemphasizes personalities and events.[16] In short, it holds that journalists should function more as social scientists.

Social science journalism may be a worthy goal. But it also requires considerable preparation time, library and research facilities, and page space or air time to do justice to complexities. There also must be an audience that has the interest as well as the leisure to read and listen. When these conditions exist, the product is a legitimate supplying of a consumer demand. When the conditions do not exist, social science journalism reflects a failure in the market economics of the news business and the degree to which reporters set their own agendas.

13. From Barry Rubin, *International News and the American Media* (Sage, 1977), p. 41. Italics added.

14. "A DEW Line on the News" in Laura Longley Babb, ed., *Of the Press, By the Press, For the Press, and Others, Too* (Houghton Mifflin, 1976), p. 233. Italics added.

15. See Diane Kiegel, June Nicholson, John Henkel, and Geri Fuller-Col, "Washington Neglected," *Quill*, vol. 66 (May 1978), p. 26; Jim Dawson and Bill Hogan, with Elizabeth Fletcher, Paula Klein, and Neal Leavitt, "The Journalism Establishment," *Washingtonian*, vol. 13 (June 1978), p. 148.

16. There is a definite division between how older and younger Washington reporters view writing about personalities. A reporter under thirty years of age says, "It's more fun to read about a divorce or how much money someone makes than to read the consumer [price] index." A reporter approaching fifty years says, "Readers want more information on health, science, and government operations, but editors continue personality-seeking, as ever." Fifty-six percent of the Washington reporters view personalities journalism as a problem, but only 29 percent of these reporters see it as a "serious" problem, with writers who work for magazines being the most outspoken. Three percent of Washington stories in newspapers and on national television are about personalities. The range for newspapers is from 1 to 10 percent; only eight of twenty-two papers use personality pieces on the front page. Chain-owned newspapers give more space to such stories, although the paper at the top of the list is an independent and the paper with the lowest percentage is chain-owned. It does not turn out that evening papers, which compete most directly with television, pay more attention to personalities; six of the eight afternoon papers in the survey are below average. Scaling the papers by geography, population area, and circulation produce no notable patterns. The figure of 3 percent seems modest compared to the degree of complaint among Washington reporters, but these stories are almost 30 percent longer than the average Washington story.

Yet even if the audience desires serious, causal, predictive reportage, there is another problem: journalism and social science are not the same. The tools of research are different; so, too, are the standards of evidence, the framework of theory, and the criteria of judgment. Paul H. Weaver points out, "Mass media organizations are not notable as centers of genuinely original thought or research."[17] Should they be? If the answer is no, this is not an argument for superficiality nor does it preclude their striving to understand and to explain.

The best journalists always have been storytellers, not theoreticians, Homers, not Aristotles. Storytelling is surely an honorable calling. Journalists have always been specialists in immediacy, chroniclers of the day. This, too, is an honorable calling. Out of the frustration of trying to deal with complexity and perhaps out of a feeling that what they do is less worthy, good journalists may become bad social scientists. The market in bad social science is already glutted.

THE NEWS business has a history of resistance to change, as have all conservative institutions. If resistance to change is bolstered by family control, will newspapers become more open to change with the rapid rise in corporate ownership? "By the mid-1980s," writes Anthony Smith, "many observers and participants expect to see most of the American daily and Sunday press in the hands of eight to ten large groups."[18] To date, the managements of chains, sensitive to charges of outside control, have stressed continuity; indeed, they bend over backwards to allow local autonomy in editorial matters. Yet bigness will affect news operations over time: in Washington, for example, bureaus allocate resources differently as they grow, tending to increase specialization.

Change in the news business usually has been in response to new technology. Many of the breakthroughs on the drawing boards—mostly use of computers—speed up production and dissemination rather than alter the nature of news or news gathering. Washington reporters increasingly compose their stories directly on visual terminal computers, thus eliminating several steps in the production process and permitting faster editing in the home office. In theory, this should make the news more up to date by allowing

17. "Mass Media and the Quality of Life," in Commission on Critical Choices for Americans, *Qualities of Life* (Lexington Books, 1976), p. 363.
18. "The Future of the Newspaper: The Waning of the Fourth Estate," *Intermedia*, vol. 6 (August 1978), p. 25.

reporters to have later deadlines. In practice, deadlines have become earlier. "I don't know why," says a former bureau chief. "They tell you that it will give us more time when the bugs are worked out, but so far this hasn't happened."

Washington news gathering also changes in response to changes in government. Government, however, changes faster than the press, which then must play catch-up. Energy as a paramount national concern is just the latest in a series of "crises" that caught the news media without appropriately trained personnel to deploy.

The press's primary response to the growth in government personnel is growth in press personnel. The number of Washington reporters has almost doubled in the past thirty years.[19] Yet this misses the point: the press continues to focus on the political government although the greatest growth in government has been in the permanent government.

The parallel growth in federal expenditures—largely funneled out of Washington through block grants and categorical aid programs—also fails to change the way the press covers government. Washington reporters are not where the bulk of federal dollars are spent. Moreover, local stories about federal programs seldom work their way back into Washington stories. The flow of news is in the other direction.

External criticism rarely has been an important force for change. The press only grudgingly (if at all) admits and corrects errors.[20] It responds more often to internal criticism. In the period of interviewing for this study, 1977–78, the Washington news corps was in a highly critical mood. Some attribute this to post-Watergate blues. In a prominent reporter's opinion, "When the news is in the doldrums we have more time to complain." News workers prefer not to repeat mistakes, but, as a general rule, neither do they much worry about mistakes until they are made. Self-correction is a kind of lurching process.

MOST Washington reporting is about breaking news: events, action taken,

19. In 1949, 621 reporters were accredited to the congressional press galleries, increasing to 746 in 1960, and 1,027 in 1979. Reporters in Washington seek accreditation to the congressional press galleries regardless of their primary beats. Thus these figures reflect the growth in the press corps, rather than growth in congressional coverage.

20. No more than twenty newspapers (out of over 1,700 in the United States) have reader's representatives or news ombudsmen; only Minnesota has a news council. See Dick Cunningham, "If you ran the Tribune . . .," Minneapolis Tribune, July 13, 1980.

words spoken, by public persons or in the name of government institutions. Despite reporters' talk about the need for in-depth coverage, the fundamental reason newswriting is likely to remain much as it is now is that news workers want it this way. Whatever leftward slant some think they detect in reporters' politics is not evident in reporters' attitudes to their work. Here they are natural conservatives, comfortable in the traditions of their craft (not unlike academics, who also have a liberal political image).

Most reporters are attracted to careers in journalism, one suspects, because it promises excitement. It provides a front-row seat at important or unusual events. It places them near important or unusual people. Reporters resist documents research for a variety of reasons, not the least being that this type of information gathering distances them from events and people; interviews and first-hand observation require proximity. Reporters resist assignments they think are dull (the departments of Agriculture, Commerce and Treasury, and the regulatory agencies). They are ambivalent about assignments that are dull but make a lot of front-page news (the Supreme Court). Variations of the word *bore* are used often by Washington journalists, as in this comment by a twenty-eight-year-old radio reporter, "Being a generalist is good in that it's nearly impossible to become bored." Boredom—or the absence of excitement—is the most uninvestigated explanation of media resource allocation, most notably of why certain topics are not covered.

In popular journalism the reporter is visible or recognized through by-lines or appearances on the television screen; the routine varies as the reporter moves from one assignment to another, often on unrelated topics; and a work product appears frequently and immediately. A veteran television correspondent says, "Reporters are in a tizzy when their faces are not on the tube at least once every few days. This is a reason why they do not want to do investigative pieces which may take months to develop. You can't blame them." An experienced newspaper reporter started to free-lance magazine articles and recalls "the intolerable pain of waiting for the pieces to appear." A reporter for a leading newspaper is assigned to a long-term project and complains of missing "the instant gratification."

Three-quarters of the Washington journalists see no serious problem in the emphasis on breaking news; a majority of newspaper and television reporters view breaking news as not being a problem at all. Those who object deeply to the dailiness of journalism usually find other avenues for their writing. Six percent of the reporters who do free-lance work say that it is because their ideas do not easily fit within the contours of daily journalism. Others leave news organizations to become independent writers. One who made this move explains, "The newspaper format doesn't lend itself to writing in depth."[21] Those who remain indicate high job satisfaction.

There is a strong element of vicarious participation, if not voyeurism, in daily journalism. David Wise, who was Washington bureau chief of the *New York Herald Tribune*, speaks of reporters spending "an awful lot of time sitting around marble corridors waiting for the grown-ups inside to tell them what's happening." He calls this "the nose-against-the-window syndrome." It is an essentially passive role. The excitement is provided by what others are doing. Reporters who will never hear a shot fired in anger wear trench coats; the wars they cover are in government and politics. The terminology is often of the racetrack, but the races are political. Some attack this stylistic habit as deliberate hyperbole,[22] but it is more charitable and more correct to view the action metaphors as reflecting the passive excitement characteristic of journalism.

The difficulties in trying to maintain the passive role should not be underestimated. David S. Broder of the *Washington Post* tells how "on every [presidential] campaign I have seen, one or more of our colleagues have strayed from the paths of righteous skepticism and become avowed, *active* promoters of the candidacy of the man they are covering."[23] For other reporters, the constant act of watching—especially of politicians—creates cynicism or frustration. Journalists like to say they will stay in the business "until my legs go." A former newsmagazine writer thinks that this is really a euphemism for "until my spirit goes." "At fifty," he says, "you may be interviewing an assistant secretary of the Interior who is fifteen years younger than you are, and you think you know a great deal more than he does." He concludes, "Reporters do not age gracefully." Fortunately, perhaps, reporting is an occupation that is easy to get out of.

21. A questionnaire was sent to twenty-five members of the Washington Independent Writers Association who had once been full-time reporters in Washington; fourteen responded. (According to their membership directory, the association has 500 members, but many are not full-time writers and others do not write about governmental affairs.) Our survey indicates that the primary reason these writers leave news organizations is to gain freedom—they appear to be uncomfortable in an organization. None claim they made the move to make more money. Most admit to having been better off financially in their former jobs, and in this sense, their work is now a subsidy to the media. Losing these often talented people on a full-time basis is the price paid for organizational maintenance in news operations.

22. See C. Anthony Broh, "Horse-Race Journalism: Reporting the Polls in the 1976 Presidential Election," *Public Opinion Quarterly*, vol. 44 (Winter 1980), pp. 514–29.

23. "Views of the Press: Political Reporters in Presidential Politics," *Washington Monthly*, vol. 1 (February 1969), p. 33. Italics added.

THERE is a personality type in journalism, or at least traits common to many reporters. The relationship between personality and journalism may be the most promising field of study for explaining why news is as it is.

Reporters are often ill at ease with abstractions. General questions, which ask for their opinions of a statement, usually are answered with anecdotes based on personal experience. In 1936 Leo C. Rosten wrote that Washington reporters' "thinking rotates around the concrete rather than the abstract. Their adjustment may be said to be that of persons to persons, rather than persons to ideas."[24] In 1955 Warren Breed wrote that "newsmen tend to analyze their society in terms of personalities, rather than institutions comprising a social and cultural system."[25] Despite their greater educational attainment (paralleling more schooling throughout the population), today's reporters have not changed as much as it might appear from a shorter perspective.

When reporters talk with each other about public affairs, they primarily exchange speculations on the prospects of a bill getting through Congress, a candidate's chances of getting elected, the personality of a cabinet officer, or who has the real power in a department. Their conversations about journalism are almost exclusively shop talk—who is getting hired and fired, who is up, who is down. Their views on professional matters usually are brought out only when news gathering itself makes news, such as the Pentagon Papers (the propriety of publishing secret documents) or Watergate (the ethics of reporters' breaking the law to get an important story). Reporters seem uncomfortable with discussions of the functions or definitions of news, and they talk still less about the structures of news organizations unless invited to a university to do so.

Washington reporters are rarely intellectuals. They are not like the news workers who produce the essays of Le Monde. The U.S. tradition in journalism is otherwise, and this is reflected in the type of people who are attracted to it. Le Monde writers might be equally startled by the amount of leg work—the mosaic of quotations and facts—that goes into the typical American newspaper story. Future study might show that reporters who have trouble with abstractions avoid doing stories that deal with complexity or do not see complexity where it exists. Some reporters fault journalism education for not teaching more theory, for being trade schools, yet it is not convincing to contend that American reporters do not have theorizing natures because

24. The Washington Correspondents, p. 240.

25. "Social Control in the Newsroom: A Functional Analysis," Social Forces, vol. 33 (May 1955), p. 331.

they were not offered the appropriate courses, especially since a majority of Washington reporters have degrees in subjects other than journalism.

Few reporters appear to be future oriented; most have a hard time responding to questions about other jobs or even assignments they would like to have "someday." When asked, many simply reply, "My present job." While this answer undoubtedly reflects satisfaction with their work, it is noteworthy that such an intelligent and upwardly mobile group pays so little attention to the future. There is an analogue in the news business, itself. No other major enterprise does so little planning: reporters and editors (who are merely ex-reporters) think in terms of the day book. Advance planning is only for major recurring events (such as elections) and anniversaries of cataclysmic happenings (presidential assassinations or stock market crashes). The reason cannot be just that news workers are so busy. A deeper cause of the press's failure to create planning mechanisms can be found in the journalist personality.

If the news media choose to build a greater planning capacity into their operations, they will have to consider where best to place this responsibility. Creating a sort of intellectual in residence, someone "above" the daily routines and processes of the organization, will work no better in the newsroom than in the White House, and for the same reason—the pace is too quick to expect meaningful involvement from a person who does not have a functional connection with events. Nor can planning for Washington coverage, except in the most general terms, be conducted at the home office in a fashion that will not be soon out of phase with the talents and schedules of reporters. The logical planner is the Washington bureau chief, who is rarely picked for this attribute.

The attraction of reporters to excitement biases news gathering in favor of certain institutions and certain types of newsmakers. Though not ideological, such biases have implications for public policy. Reporters prefer to cover the Senate rather than the House of Representatives; the State Department, rather than the regulatory agencies; politics rather than management.

These preferences, reporters feel, are encouraged by their home offices, in part because of the prestige in having an organization's own people at the major centers of news. One effect of this is that papers often are provided with several versions of the same story—from their own reporters, the wires, and supplemental news services. The overwhelming majority of Washington reporters (70 percent) argue that multiple stories create a form of competition among reporters. Although over half agree that the lack of coverage of regulatory agencies is a serious problem, they would not move reporters from other areas but would hire more staff and expand the news hole. Whether this is economically feasible is not a concern of reporters, who seldom have any interest in the business side of their industry. A magazine editor (previously a Washington reporter) says, "I doubt very many reporters have ever read the annual report of the company they work for."

In an information system based on personal contacts, the affinity between reporters and sources helps shape the content of news. Some news sources are automatic—people who must be approached because of the positions they hold. But otherwise, reporters seek news sources they prefer to be with, and these are overwhelmingly in the political world, both elected and appointed. True, Washington is the political capital and these sources fill reporters' professional needs. But above this, there is the mesh of personalities: reporters and politicians live in the same time frame, at the cutting edge of the moment; they are storytellers, they are ill at ease with abstractions, and both groups are in a business of instant gratification, variety, excitement. Politicians often criticize reporters for having characteristics they too have, such as an inability to focus on one subject for a long time. And there is a solipsistic quality about both reporters and politicians, their sense that nothing can exist if it is not part of their own experiences. They like each other—and hate each other—because they are so much alike. Both, I think, are optimists; if asked to recount the past, they would stress "the good times."[26] Yet they engage in occupations that are basically dissimilar. Politics is active, reporting is passive. The joining is symbiotic.

Some other news sources almost seem to repel reporters. Civil servants, for example, have strange ways; they even speak a strange tongue called bureaucratese. By not connecting with the permanent government, reporters reinforce the lack of a historical memory in news gathering. This is buttressed by what they read, by their limited use of documents in their work, and by their relationships, both personal and professional, with the political government. Both politicians and reporters, as James Fallows points out, "imagine that the world of public life is created anew each day, or at most every four years."[27]

The attraction and repellence of personalities suggest a reason why

26. Similarities between reporters and politicians in Great Britain are noted by Jeremy Tunstall, *The Westminster Lobby Correspondents* (London: Routledge and Kegan Paul, 1970), p. 24.

27. "The President and the Press," *Washington Monthly*, vol. 11 (October 1979), p. 17.

Washington journalists do not pay much attention to matters of implementation, but their failure to delve deeply into what happens to a program after it has been turned over to the permanent government cannot be entirely explained by a theory of polar personalities. Reporters and civil servants may not mix, but there are also other factors that work against sustained coverage. Implementation often takes place in the field, outside the purview of Washington reporters. It is difficult to measure. It is often a documents story. Implementation is not breaking news unless public officials choose to make it so. (Process stories, which have many of the same characteristics, are somewhat better covered, probably because they more often deal with politics.)

A single image of reporters can be pushed too far. (There are differences, too, among politicians.) Some reporters do excel at documents research—I. F. Stone being a notable example—and others can spend months happily ferreting out a story. Those who write substantive books (as opposed to accounts of "presidents who have known me") obviously are capable of deferred gratification. The corps of Washington reporters is made up of 1,200 individuals, not all of whom will conform to a prototype.

THE JOURNALISTIC personality and the quasi-professional nature of journalism have produced an unusual personnel pattern in Washington reporting. There is a steady outflow of experienced journalists: 38 percent are in their thirties, 25 percent in their forties, 16 percent over fifty. Relatively few make it their life's work.

Not requiring academic credentials or certification, journalism is easy to drift into. It is regulated only by supply and demand. Also, it is an occupation that prepares people for other things, especially in Washington. So reporters leave journalism in part because they have other opportunities.

But that reporters want to leave has most to do with the journalistic personality.[28] The excitement wears off. "Things that might seem exciting, front-page stories, scoops, are more satisfying to a young person than after one has done it for the hundredth time," says an independent writer, a former Washington reporter. "Bringing down their second president will not be as exciting to Woodward and Bernstein. Watergate, of course, would be

28. Other theories contend that reporters drop out because the pay is low or the energy demands are high. This may be true in local journalism, with its greater accent on "unscheduled" events—fires and crime. Neither of these facts apply in Washington, where the salary levels are at least middle class and the hours worked are not out of line with the compensation received.

exciting to anyone, but I'm talking about the run-of-the-mill story. The twentieth year covering the Hill is going to be less exciting than the third." Journalism may well be—as it is often said—a young person's profession, but not because of the stamina needed to do the work. Creeping repetition is the most important cause for seeking other employment.

Washington-based columnist Stanley Karnow claims, "Journalism is the only profession in which you can stay an adolescent all your life." The best reporters never lose this sense of excitement, often associated with youth. Many of these zestful older reporters cover national politics; they are, in this, also like certain successful politicians—Hubert Humphrey comes to mind— who find endless fascination in campaigning, long after others have lost their enthusiasm.

The typical career pattern of reporters is financially advantageous to their employers. There is a need for lots of reporters, not many editors and columnists, fewer publishers. It is like the military. Wars are fought by battalions of privates and a command post of generals. In wartime the military can conscript the young; in peacetime it can discharge the excess. An army keeps its shape by hiring and firing without regard to union contracts or the profit motive. Journalism, however, is a private enterprise in a labor-intensive industry. One reason news organizations are so profitable is that the foot soldiers voluntarily leave before seniority sets in and makes them more expensive. At the same time, government, industry, unions, and public affairs organizations are advantaged by the movement of reporters out of journalism: what journalists acquire on the job—the ability to be good observers, knowledge of a wide variety of institutions and programs, and writing skills—become assets to other employers, the training costs having been absorbed by the news media.

Given that rotating reporters to other locations is the exception, the natural pattern of departures from Washington journalism provides the press corps a degree of fluidity, of circulation, it would not otherwise have. This may be the only part of the system that counters the sense of isolation, of being out of touch. If experience produces better reporters, the pattern is costly, but with higher turnover rates in Congress and on congressional committee staffs, the benefits of longstanding contacts and tenure are eroding. In addition, a countertrend is at work: specialist reporters are less likely to leave journalism, so with greater specialization, the Washington press corps will become older and more stable, will be more costly to maintain and have less room for entering reporters.

Until then, however, the least committed and the least motivated leave journalism altogether. Other reporters become editorial writers, columnists, and independent writers. And in many cases—because editors and publishers are paid better—good print reporters are moved out of reporting into administration on the dubious assumption that the skills necessary to be a good reporter are the same as those needed in a good editor or publisher. Television, on the other hand, maintains separate tracks for news gatherers and news processors (producers do not get paid more).

THE QUASI-PROFESSIONAL nature of journalism raises questions about what is the best training for Washington reporters. Prevailing sociological theory is that an occupation becomes a profession when technical skill and complexity reach a point where performance can be evaluated only by peers. Under this definition, a profession of generalists is not possible.

The content of Washington journalism becomes increasingly technical. Reporters must understand complexity and must make it understandable to their consumers. Yet specialized training is the antithesis of mass communication. Medical and law schools, for example, hardly are designed to narrow the knowledge gap between users and producers. During an extended stay in most graduate programs, students absorb the worst jargon of the disciplines they seek to master; moreover, they often become obsessed with their own seriousness, if not solemnity, hardly a mind-set that future reporters will find useful in their work. But so long as supply exceeds demand, employers will use possession of advanced degrees as a criterion in hiring, even if the training is only of marginal value to the work. Major news organizations, at the moment, lean toward hiring Washington reporters with graduate degrees in specialized subjects. They assume that the craft skills of journalism can be successfully acquired on the job, probably truer in the print media than in television.

A majority of the Washington press corps do not have degrees in journalism. But if majoring in journalism has not been a liability in getting ahead, neither has it been an asset. There is no positive correlation between journalism education and prestige beats, employment in influential organizations, promotion to bureau chief, or other forms of advancement in the world of Washington newswork. Yet it would be a mistake for schools of journalism to try to produce instant specialists. They cannot turn themselves into combination law school, medical school, department of economics, and so on. A tenured faculty cannot adjust to the constantly changing specialized needs of the news business, where one season demands expertise in space technology, the next, expertise in energy.

Preparing reporters to deal with complexity should mean teaching research procedures that go beyond the interview technique. The press continues in this documents-laden society to rely on oral research tools. Information slips by—particularly the knowledge stored in computers—because news workers are unwilling or unable to take advantage of it. Says one Washington bureau chief, "Not many reporters are good at [documents] research. They think they are, but they're not. Most reporters don't know how to compile a financial record on an individual because they've never been taught. Investigative reporting in Washington is through the transom. Somebody drops something on you, and if it's good stuff you win a prize. It's surprising how little research was involved in the Watergate stories. Did the press trace the laundering of money? No, it was someone in the FBI, who then leaked it."

The press always will be a reactive institution, but its reaction time to new knowledge need not be so delayed. The most promising way to keep in phase with shifting specialized needs is through midcareer education. Yet the news industry has shown only modest interest. It would be hard to find a news operation that rationally sets out to retrain employees to fit its changing needs. Says the bureau chief of a highly profitable and respected operation, "My paper has a historic prejudice against giving sabbaticals. It's not impossible to get one. But the reporter would have to have a lot of clout." Organizations have not even taken full advantage of existing educational programs, usually offered by universities at less than cost, and, in effect, a form of outside subsidy to the news media.

OF ALL the problems of Washington news gathering, the one that reporters find most serious has been given the name pack journalism. Only 8 percent of the press do not feel it is a problem. The responses isolate two separate conditions: one, reporters are packed together, that is, they cover the same events, such as presidential news conferences, rather than venturing out on their own; two, they arrive at pack decisions, often based on pooling information. Eugene McCarthy once compared the press to blackbirds on a telephone line. One flies off, the others fly off; one comes back, the others come back. All in a row. It is the second condition that reporters consider more troubling, for it implies that they do not form independent judgments or even that they are somehow cheating.

Yet how different could their judgments be when—as Timothy Crouse notes—the reporters live in the same city, use the same sources, belong to the same professional groups, and swear by the same omens? He concludes of those covering presidential campaigns: "They arrived at their answers just as independently as a class of honest seventh graders using the same geometry text—they did not have to cheat off each other to come up with the same answer."[29] Crouse is right in stressing common vantage point rather than socioeconomic similarities. When women or blacks are on the beats that most often produce pack journalism, they are not immune. From the same perspective, there is one view. It is a matter of optics.

Still, there is more than meets the eye. Editors wonder—perhaps properly— when their reporters too often see events in a very different light from other reporters. Presumably there are "right" answers. And if the majority answer turns out to be wrong, there is comfort for the reporters in knowing that they were not wrong alone. What occupation wishes to maximize risk? Even Hollywood stuntmen take precautions to survive. When the work has to be done very fast, when events are subject to different interpretations, when participants are unknown or not available, when the situation is complicated, it is useful to have colleagues to compare impressions with. But unlike doctors, for whom it is a matter of pride to make the same diagnosis, reporters sharing diagnoses feel almost conspiratorial. They prefer to think of themselves as lone rangers, and even having research assistants creates problems for their self-image. They take precautions, then feel uneasy. (The great politicians whom they admire are notorious risk takers.) Again, one wonders about this as part of the journalist personality.

Of course, the press corps could be concerned about pack journalism not because their individualism is in doubt but because it has produced mistaken perceptions so often. In recent presidential politics the press saw Edmund Muskie as the frontrunner in 1972, discounting George McGovern; Henry Jackson as the frontrunner in 1976, discounting Jimmy Carter. It is debatable whether their shared perceptions were any different from their individual perceptions, but limiting the number of perspectives does limit the opportunities to see things differently. Which suggests the criticism of the other form of pack journalism.

Is not something wrong when all the firemen rush to the same fire? In theory at least, Americans, including news workers, are offended by inefficiency; the United States pioneered time-and-motion studies. Adjusting resources, however, requires an adjuster controlling where reporters are

29. *The Boys on the Bus* (Random House, 1973), p. 44.

located and what they are covering; and this, of course, is exactly what news workers wish to avoid. Instead, Washington news gathering is procedural pluralism, or "let a hundred flowers bloom."[30]

The results are that the sum of Washington reporting does not add up to the universe of government activities; it is excessive in some areas, nonexistent in others. This cannot accurately be called a system if a system is defined as an arrangement that molds the parts into an organic whole. Rather, Washington news is produced by a large number of small, fiercely competitive units, each functioning independently and without regard for how its operation affects other news-gathering agencies or the totality of information that reaches the public.[31]

When an event is public—such as a trial—and all reporters must rely on the same equally available resources, procedural pluralism is hard to justify. A rule of thumb should be, Can a reporter get information that will not be available to the wire services and reported as adequately by them? Washington reporters rarely criticize the quality of AP and UPI stories, as they once did. In practice, however, there are few Washington stories on which different reporters do not produce some different information. (Because the popular media often use the same lead stories, resources appear to be more redundant than they actually are.) Only a handful of the press corps waits at the White House or travels on the campaign buses. While some could be moved to other assignments without diminishing the news flow, this would not greatly expand Washington coverage. Only at the television networks is a substantial portion of resources devoted to overlapping stories. To operate otherwise would require pooling arrangements on all major beats, which, though it would free reporters to cover other stories, would produce uniform coverage of the top news.[32] Would this be an improvement? Duplicating resources at least leaves open the possibility that correspondents, spurred on by the competition, will do a better job. But the most important effect of procedural pluralism is as a check on the influence of any one news gatherer.

30. Some news organizations claim they need procedural pluralism because of their unique style. While it is true that a New York Times account would not fit comfortably in the New York Daily News, or vice versa, more often Washington print reportage is interchangeable, while television reporters can switch from one network to another without adjusting their style. For a discussion of procedural pluralism in another context, see James Douglas and Aaron Wildavsky, "Introduction," in Russell Sage Foundation, Annual Report 1961–1977, pp. 44–45.

31. See Tom Wicker, On Press (Viking, 1978), p. 18. The growth of supplemental news services, for example, might bankrupt one of the traditional wire services, but where in the nonsystem of the news industry will the consequences of this development be carefully considered?

32. The case for greater use of television pooling on routine stories is made by Fred W. Friendly, "The University Lecture in Journalism," University of Michigan, March 10, 1971.

THIS study provides new answers to the question, Who is deciding what is news? The findings, if surprising, are less so when the study's vantage point is recalled. Many recent attempts to explain the news media have been directed at the top, recounting life and times in corporate headquarters and home offices. In this study the sightings were taken at the bottom, looking at the worker in the field, usually far from headquarters. Things, including organizations, look different from different angles.

The news business also may look different from a nonjournalist's perspective. For example, Washington reporters bridle at home-office requests for stories, although we find that these requests consume a very small percentage of their time. They worry, too, about bureaucratization in their operations. News organizations are bureaucracies, of course, and they may become more bureaucratic as they grow larger, but they are considerably less hierarchical than other types of enterprises of comparable size. To news workers, newswork seems to be much more controlled from the top than it appears to an outsider.

Moreover, many recent studies concentrate on national operations—television networks, weekly newsmagazines, newspapers of reputation beyond their immediate circulation areas—and ignore the many smaller operations whose reporters and collective impact play an important role in the dissemination of information. Centralized control is a by-product of the technology of television and is part of the basic design at the newsmagazines, where reports from the outposts are blended into a finished product. Prestige organizations often grant the least autonomy to their workers (and thus prestige reporters at prestige organizations may be the most conflicted; they are also the most likely to write books explaining the media).

A conclusion that the more national the character of the news operation, the greater the home-office control—while generally true—misses a key point: the nature of news gathering vests considerable autonomy in all news gatherers.[33] And the nature of Washington news gathering (regardless of an organization's size) adds to their freedom. Reporters' autonomy is greater (1) the greater their distance from their home offices; (2) the more prestige they have; (3) the longer they have worked at their jobs; (4) the greater their specialized knowledge; (5) the more complex the news they cover; (6) the more sources they grant anonymity; and (7) the less revenue related

---

33. Autonomy has been observed even in local journalism. Lee Sigelman's study of two Southern newspapers notes that there was "some degree of functional autonomy at even the lowest reportorial levels. Indeed, reporters exercise significant power in shaping both their own roles and the operation of the entire organization." See his "Reporting the News: An Organizational Analysis," *American Journal of Sociology*, vol. 79 (July 1973), p. 142.

their stories. Using these formulations, the Washington reporter with least autonomy is a young person on general assignment for a television network; the most autonomous is an older specialist reporter for a noninfluential newspaper.

This survey shows that Washington reporters initiate the vast majority of their stories and that the stories get good placement and hardly any editing. When Washington is also the home office, the reporters' autonomy is lessened, but in general, Washington reporters are freer of supervision than any other type of news gatherer save the foreign correspondent. Washington reporters are, almost by definition, the stars of their organizations. Few are under thirty years old. Their reporting is becoming more specialized and the news more complex. Sources are granted anonymity more than in other parts of the country. And unlike stories about automobiles, real estate, or food, news from Washington is rarely related to an operation's receipts and hence not as susceptible to management's influence.

True, constraints are imposed on reporters by the type of organization they work for (copy must fit time, space, style, and technical requirements); by the beat system (they can gather information only within prescribed areas); by the parameters of permissible news (defined for them by tradition, libel law, and consumer acceptance); and by profitability or other management considerations that determine the amount of money they can have for travel and expenses. Other limitations are self-imposed and can be ignored, but not without cost: if they treat a news source roughly, they could endanger their access to news; if they fail to take into account what competitors are writing, they could endanger their standing within their own organization. Moreover, news events are largely determined by natural forces or governments, beyond the control of either editor or reporter. It is not the journalist who calls the press conference, casts the vote, or pulls the trigger. (Still, the *form* of human events increasingly adjusts to the needs of the media, and these accommodations affect the *nature* of the events. Only the most unperceptive news workers believe that they function merely as flies on the wall and that their presence does not affect the behavior of newsmakers.)

Yet to the degree that the media decide what is Washington news, the decisions are most often made in the field, not in executive suites. The reporters, collectively, cover what interests them, and do not cover what does not interest them. In public administration it is said, "Let me write the option paper, I'll let you make the decisions."[34] In newswork, organizations

34. The aphorism is attributed to Herbert Kaufman.

make the decisions (What will be the front page lead? Will the evening news be expanded to an hour?), but day to day, the options on the content of news are written by Washington reporters.

Headquarters allows control to drift out of its hands in part because the events that interest or fail to interest Washington reporters are roughly the same events that interest or do not interest editors. When there is a conflict, editors probably could get their way. (A participant in a shake-up by the *Chicago Sun-Times* of its Washington bureau says, "It reminds us all who cracks the whip.") But most editors do not bother, for a variety of reasons— not caring very much, not knowing very much, being too busy, deferring to experts, wanting to maintain morale. Probably the most frequent reason is inertia. It is in the interests of reporters to leave as vague as possible the exact balance of autonomy and control.

The autonomy of Washington reporters has consequences for what will be covered. The gradual shifting from regional news, for example, is a direct result of reporters' freedom of choice. Editors—at least so they say—would like more stories about how government in Washington affects their circulation areas, but they do not get them because the Washington press corps prefers to write about other matters. What reporters do not want to cover is not necessarily what consumers need not be informed about—economics, for example. Conversely, there are subjects—notably international affairs—that reporters cover extensively despite survey evidence that consumers are less interested than they are.

Reporters spend relatively little time in their circulation areas once they take up residence in Washington. Their travels, while extensive, are always on specific assignments, always rushed, often to places that do not help them stay in touch with readers. Consumers rarely write them. Those who do, reporters feel, are not representative. Home offices rarely share unpublished letters to the editor or the results of consumer surveys. As Washington journalism becomes more specialized, reporters are hired for subject-area expertise rather than knowledge of the city in which their reporting appears. Consumers are even easier than editors to forget. In their isolated world, reporters find their satisfactions and status from their peers in the press corps. How to break the isolation is a problem that reporters and their organizations recognize but seem unwilling to seriously address, partly because the answers can be expensive for management and uncomfortable for labor.

WHAT has been happening, perhaps slowly and subtly enough to escape broad notice, is that over time the proprietors gave up control of content to the editors, and the editors, in turn, are losing control to the reporters.[35] At least this is the way it appears from Washington to this observer. Three phenomena are at the root of this shift: the changing ownership of news organizations, their growth, and the professional status of editorial workers.

The steady movement is from politically motivated newspaper publishers— the William Randolph Hearsts and Robert R. McCormicks in the United States, Lord Beaverbrooks and Cecil Kings in Great Britain—to the corporate managers. The new breed is not concerned with ideology. Indeed, a highly politicized product can be bad for business. To a lesser degree—because they are designed to be interpretive—this is even the case at the newsmagazines in the post–Henry Luce era. The television networks, unlike their news divisions, are always run by nonjournalists, which creates frictions but does not negate the general rule. (Reporters do not worry that media corporations will use their properties for political purposes.[36] Reporters also know that this is the sort of threat that they are very good at turning into very bad publicity, and public corporations have a fierce aversion to bad publicity.)

The news business is highly profitable, and the proprietors' implicit bargain with their reporters makes it even more profitable. Reporters have fewer management prerogatives than workers of comparable status in most other industries. At the same time, Washington reporters could cite almost no examples of management imposing editorial judgments on their copy. This is a trade-off that seems to satisfy both management and labor. Reporters, who are not business people and care little even for the business of their own business, want to appear in print or on the air; the new proprietors, who are or become business people, want to make a profit. Each side gets what it most wants. This is not to say that reporters are exploited or that proprietors take no pride in their product. On the contrary. Reporters are well paid by the standards and expectations they set for themselves when they chose journalism as a career, and proprietors, especially in monopoly situations, usually make greater investments than are necessary to retain consumers and

35. A similar trend has been noted in Great Britain by John Beavan (Lord Ardwick), the former London editor of the *Manchester Guardian*, who writes, "Political power began moving away from publishers towards the editors of some popular newspapers; and away from the once all-powerful editors of some quality newspapers towards their writers." See his "Commissions, Committees and the Craft of Journalism," *Political Quarterly*, vol. 49 (January–March 1978), p. 72.

36. There are worries about press credibility, however, when media companies also own other types of businesses. See Stephen Hess, "The News Business: Staying Credible," *Baltimore Sun*, May 12, 1980.

advertisers. Whether this will change if the news business should become less profitable is a question that rightly worries editorial workers.

As news organizations grow bigger, the reporters gain greater control over content. Reporters think the opposite happens, but this is because they confuse red tape with control. As the organizations that they work for get larger and more far-flung, reporters will have to learn to live with more bureaucratic management. There will be elaborate travel vouchers to fill out; bureau chiefs, and perhaps even reporters, will have to prepare detailed budgets—and these should give news workers a sufficiency to complain about. But if they look closely they will find that there is less interference with the gathering and reporting of news. In Washington, bureaus of newspaper chains have more independence than bureaus of independent newspapers; regional reporters for multiple papers have more independence than regional reporters for a single newspaper. Control weakens as the distance increases from top to bottom. Reporters write about this when it occurs in government, but do not relate span-of-control doctrines to their own work.

The reporters' control over content also increases in direct proportion to their rise in professional status. The professionalism movement was designed to correct the abuses of yellow journalism in the late nineteenth century. From this laudable beginning the press has created for itself most of the trappings of a profession. Once an occupation is accepted as a profession, the only acceptable controls are self-controls and peer-controls; those not trained or otherwise qualified are not entitled to pass judgment. The increasing expectation of reporters that their stories will appear as written is founded on professional virtue, not on property rights.

The editorial independence of reporters may be more pronounced in Washington than in other locations. And even in Washington there are wide differences among organizations and types of organizations. The overall impression, however, is that Washington news gathering fragments the power of the media, while at the same time it shifts decisions on what is news and how it should be covered to the reporters.

APPENDIX

Statistics

THE STATISTICAL information that follows generally corresponds to the sequence in which subjects are discussed in the text. Chapter titles are included in the titles of the tables. However, data often appear in more than one chapter. Table titles and page numbers are

Key to Tables

Number of responses is the sum from which percentages may be converted to counts. (Percentages are rounded to the nearest tenth and so may not add to 100.) Unless otherwise indicated, data from the telephone survey (number = 194) are not included for categories with fewer than eight cases, and data from the merged telephone-survey/mailed-questionnaire (number = 476) are not included for categories with fewer than twenty responses. This explains, for example, why some tables do not include the breakdown by race—there were too few black respondents. In some categories the number of responses exceeds the number of reporters; for example, many of them had more than one field of study in college and many have more than one beat.

Race. One respondent, coded as a black, listed himself as a member of a racial minority, unspecified.

Urban/rural. *Urban* is defined as a standard metropolitan statistical area. According to the U.S. Bureau of the Census, "Generally speaking an SMSA consists of a county or group of counties containing at least one city (or twin cities) having a population of 50,000 or more plus adjacent counties which are metropolitan in character and are economically and socially integrated with the central city." Reporters were placed in urban or rural categories on the basis of present SMSAs, which may not have been so designated when they were living there. This category does not total 100 percent because some reporters have mixed urban/rural backgrounds and others were raised in foreign countries.

Regional influence. This scale combines the state(s) in which reporters spent their childhood years with the state(s) in which they went to college as undergraduates. *Northeast* includes Maine, New Hampshire, Vermont, Massachusetts, Rhode Island, Connecticut, New York, New Jersey, and Pennsylvania. *North Central* includes Ohio, Indiana, Illinois, Michigan, Wisconsin, Minnesota, Iowa, Missouri, North Dakota, South Dakota, Nebraska, and Kansas. *South* includes Delaware, Maryland, the District of Columbia, Virginia, West Virginia, North Carolina, South Carolina, Georgia, Florida, Kentucky, Tennessee, Alabama, Mississippi, Arkansas, Louisiana, Oklahoma, and Texas. *West* includes Montana, Idaho, Wyoming, Colorado, New Mexico, Arizona, Utah, Nevada, Washington, Oregon, California, Alaska, and Hawaii.

College selectivity. This rating system was devised by James Cass and Max Birnbaum, *Comparative Guide to American Colleges*, 8th ed. (Harper and Row, 1977), pp. 741–46. Their two top categories are here combined, and schools they do not list are rated *not selective*. The ranking is based on "the percentage of applicants accepted by the college, the average test scores of recent freshman classes, the ranking of recent freshmen in their high school classes, and other related data" (ibid., p. xix).

Fields of study. Humanities/liberal arts includes English, literature, creative writing, history, political science, government, other humanities and social sciences, and general liberal arts. Science/technology includes mathematics, the physical and biological sciences, agriculture, economics, business, education, law, medicine, and accountancy. Journalism/communication is the third category. A number of respondents listed more than one field of study.

Chains/independents. Reporters were coded as working for independent newspapers if the Washington operation they work for services only one outlet, even though the parent corporation may own more than one newspaper or the operation's reportage may be sold to other news organizations. For example, reporters for the *Washington Post*, the *New York Times*, and the *Los Angeles Times* were counted in the independent newspaper category.

Influentials. This scale is based on the reading and listening habits of the Washington press corps. The following organizations are found by this scale to be influential: the *Washington Post*, the *New York Times*, the *Washington Star*, the *Wall Street Journal*, *Time*, *Newsweek*, *U.S. News & World Report*, the Associated Press, the United Press International, the American Broadcasting Company, the Columbia Broadcasting System, and the National Broadcasting Company.

Beat. Related assignments are combined in some cases. Diplomacy includes defense and national security; science includes space; energy includes environment; economics includes business; domestic includes agriculture, civil rights, consumer affairs, education, health, labor, transportation, and urban affairs. The designation class A general assignment indicates that reporters choose their own stories without being confined to a specific beat, while class B general assignment reporters are assigned stories on an ad hoc basis. The regional beat is the coverage of Washington news that affects a particular locale.

Specialist/generalist. This designation is based on reporters' self-evaluations; that is, their responses to the question, "Do you consider yourself a specialist or a generalist?"

Table 1. Work: Job Satisfaction
Percent

Characteristic of reporter	Number of responses	Satisfaction rating			
		Very satisfied	Fairly satisfied	Somewhat dissatisfied	Very dissatisfied
Male	140	40.0	44.3	13.6	2.1
Female	52	40.4	44.2	13.5	1.9
Age					
20–29	49	34.7	42.9	22.4	0.0
30–39	69	40.6	46.4	8.7	4.3
40–49	53	41.5	43.4	13.2	1.9
50 and over	21	47.6	42.9	9.5	0.0
Employer					
Wire service	17	41.2	29.4	23.5	5.9
Network television	20	45.0	45.0	10.0	0.0
Radio	18	50.0	22.2	22.2	5.6
Magazine	10	50.0	40.0	10.0	0.0
Specialized publication	41	29.3	61.0	7.3	2.4
Newspaper	76	40.8	43.4	14.5	1.3
Influential	63	39.7	46.0	12.7	1.6
Noninfluential	129	40.3	43.4	14.0	2.3
Beat					
White House	8	50.0	50.0	0.0	0.0
Congress	15	40.0	40.0	20.0	0.0
Diplomacy	15	46.7	46.7	0.0	6.7
Class A general assignment	10	40.0	50.0	10.0	0.0
Law	14	28.6	28.6	35.7	7.1
Economics	15	46.7	46.7	6.7	0.0
Energy	13	38.5	46.2	15.4	0.0
Regional	27	25.9	48.1	22.2	3.7
Domestic	17	35.3	58.8	5.9	0.0
Class B general assignment	26	34.6	53.8	7.7	3.8
Specialist	75	45.3	48.0	6.7	0.0
Generalist	117	36.8	41.9	17.9	3.4
Politics					
Liberal	53	35.8	39.6	18.9	5.7
Middle-of-road/independent	49	38.8	49.0	10.2	2.0
Conservative	25	40.0	52.0	8.0	0.0
Total news corps	192	40.1	44.3	13.5	2.1

Table 2. Work: Average Level of Disagreements with Home Office
Scale 0–3[a]

Characteristic of reporter	Type of disagreement									
	Story length	Story placement	Time to write	Story requests	Story angle	Writing style	Beat/ assignment	Money/ travel	Political slant	Expenses
Male	1.7	1.4	1.2	1.2	0.9	0.9	0.8	0.5	0.3	0.4
Female	1.7	1.2	1.3	1.2	0.9	0.9	0.9	0.5	0.5	0.4
White	1.7	1.3	1.2	1.2	0.9	0.9	0.8	0.5	0.3	0.4
Black	1.7	1.0	0.7	0.5	1.0	1.0	1.0	0.0	0.7	0.0
Age										
20–29	1.5	1.3	1.5	1.5	1.1	1.0	0.8	0.6	0.5	0.5
30–39	1.8	1.4	1.4	1.2	1.0	0.9	0.9	0.6	0.3	0.4
40–49	1.8	1.4	0.9	1.0	0.7	0.8	0.7	0.4	0.2	0.2
50 and over	1.6	1.1	1.0	1.3	1.0	0.6	0.5	0.3	0.2	0.3
Employer										
Wire service	1.9	0.9	1.3	1.3	0.9	1.2	0.8	0.4	0.2	0.5
Network television	2.7	1.4	1.3	1.5	0.8	0.7	1.1	0.2	0.3	0.4
Radio	1.8	0.9	1.5	1.3	1.1	0.8	0.9	0.6	0.4	0.5
Magazine	1.5	1.0	1.8	1.2	1.7	0.7	1.1	0.3	1.0	0.2
Specialized publication	1.0	0.9	1.1	1.0	1.0	1.1	0.7	0.7	0.4	0.5
Newspaper	1.8	1.6	1.1	1.1	0.7	0.8	0.7	0.6	0.2	0.3
Influential	2.1	1.2	1.4	1.2	0.9	0.9	0.9	0.3	0.3	0.3
Noninfluential	1.5	1.4	1.1	1.2	0.9	0.9	0.8	0.6	0.4	0.4

Beat

White House	2.9	1.0	1.7	1.0	0.9	0.9	0.9	0.1	0.3	0.4
Congress	1.4	0.9	1.2	1.4	1.4	0.6	0.6	0.7	0.4	0.2
Diplomacy	2.0	1.4	1.4	1.1	0.9	0.9	0.9	0.5	0.1	0.2
Class A general assignment	2.0	2.1	1.0	0.9	1.0	0.8	0.9	0.7	0.1	0.7
Law	2.3	1.7	1.4	1.4	1.4	1.3	1.4	0.5	0.6	0.5
Economics	1.5	1.0	1.6	1.3	0.8	1.1	0.6	0.3	0.2	0.6
Energy	0.8	0.5	1.0	0.8	0.5	0.5	0.6	0.9	0.1	0.5
Regional	1.3	2.0	1.3	1.4	0.7	0.8	0.7	0.5	0.2	0.4
Domestic	1.5	1.1	0.7	0.8	0.7	0.6	0.3	0.1	0.2	0.1
Class B general assignment	2.2	1.6	1.0	1.6	1.0	1.2	1.1	0.6	0.4	0.2
Specialist	1.6	1.1	1.2	1.2	0.9	0.8	0.7	0.4	0.4	0.4
Generalist	1.8	1.5	1.3	1.2	0.9	0.9	0.9	0.6	0.3	0.4

Politics

Liberal	1.6	1.4	1.3	1.4	1.2	1.0	0.8	0.6	0.4	0.4
Middle-of-road/independent	1.6	1.5	1.5	1.3	1.0	1.0	0.9	0.6	0.4	0.4
Conservative	1.8	1.1	1.1	1.2	0.7	0.9	1.0	0.4	0.2	0.3
Total news corps	1.7	1.3	1.2	1.2	0.9	0.9	0.8	0.5	0.4	0.4
Number of responses	(174)	(151)	(173)	(165)	(174)	(172)	(164)	(170)	(173)	(175)

a. Reporters rated each disagreement, 0 = never, 1 = seldom, 2 = sometimes, 3 = often. The average of all disagreements is 0.92, or less than "seldom."

Table 3. Work: Editing by Home Office
Percent

Characteristic of reporter	Number of responses	Amount of editing		
		None	Minor	Substantial
Age				
20–29	110	35.5	60.0	4.6
30–39	186	53.2	44.1	2.7
40–49	103	51.5	44.7	3.9
50 and over	74	68.9	31.1	0.0
Employer				
Wire service	33	24.2	72.7	3.0
Network television	40	92.5	7.5	0.0
Magazine	13	38.5	53.9	7.7
Specialized publication	52	23.1	71.2	5.8
Newspaper	291	50.5	46.7	2.8
Influential	161	42.9	54.0	3.1
Noninfluential	304	55.6	41.5	3.0
Beat				
White House	27	66.7	33.3	0.0
Congress	39	56.4	38.5	5.1
Diplomacy	31	51.6	48.4	0.0
Class A general assignment	55	63.6	34.6	1.8
Law	17	47.1	52.9	0.0
Economics	46	28.3	67.4	4.4
Regional	108	61.1	37.0	1.9
Domestic	40	45.0	47.5	7.5
Class B general assignment	49	59.2	40.8	0.0
Total news corps	465	51.2	45.8	3.0

Table 4. Work: Average Hours and Stories per Week
Figures in parentheses are number of responses

Characteristic of reporter	Hours worked[a]	Hours spent on stories not "panning out"	Number of stories filed[b]	Percent of hard news stories filed
Male	42.9	2.6	7.1	80.0
	(193)	(191)	(191)	(177)
Female	40.1	3.3	6.5	82.8
	(44)	(44)	(44)	(40)
White	42.4	2.7	6.9	81.5
	(225)	(223)	(223)	(205)
Black	40.5	4.9	8.7	66.7
	(10)	(10)	(10)	(9)
Age				
20–29	42.6	4.5	8.6	80.6
	(50)	(50)	(50)	(48)
30–39	42.5	1.9	6.5	81.1
	(92)	(91)	(91)	(85)
40–49	43.5	2.3	5.8	82.6
	(56)	(55)	(55)	(48)
50 and over	40.1	3.3	7.7	78.3
	(39)	(39)	(39)	(36)
Employer				
Wire service	42.0	2.4	10.3	91.4
	(18)	(18)	(18)	(17)
Network television	44.9	3.7	9.6	73.1
	(21)	(21)	(21)	(19)
Magazine	47.2	2.6	3.8	77.8
	(17)	(16)	(16)	(10)
Specialized publication	36.3	2.6	4.8	78.6
	(33)	(33)	(33)	(31)
Newspaper	42.8	2.3	6.1	83.3
	(127)	(126)	(126)	(119)
Influential	45.1	2.6	7.1	84.7
	(93)	(93)	(93)	(81)
Noninfluential	40.5	2.7	6.8	77.4
	(141)	(139)	(139)	(133)
Beat				
White House	41.6	1.8	7.1	76.8
	(20)	(20)	(20)	(16)
Congress	41.7	2.9	6.6	88.5
	(18)	(18)	(18)	(17)
Diplomacy	40.8	2.5	6.5	87.8
	(17)	(17)	(17)	(14)

Table 4 *(continued)*

Characteristic of reporter	Hours worked[a]	Hours spent on stories not "panning out"	Number of stories filed[b]	Percent of hard news stories filed
Beat (continued)				
Class A general assignment	47.5	3.0	5.9	80.9
	(27)	(26)	(26)	(24)
Law	44.2	2.0	7.2	90.9
	(9)	(9)	(9)	(8)
Economics	41.6	3.1	7.1	87.9
	(16)	(15)	(15)	(15)
Regional	42.5	3.6	9.1	78.9
	(39)	(39)	(39)	(39)
Domestic	41.9	2.7	8.3	86.7
	(26)	(26)	(26)	(23)
Class B general assignment	43.2	2.7	6.3	68.7
	(28)	(28)	(28)	(26)
Politics	42.5	0.6	2.5	. . .
	(8)	(8)	(8)	
Total news corps	42.4	2.8	7.0	80.5
Number of responses	(237)	(235)	(235)	(217)

a. Figures are adjusted for incomplete logs.
b. Incomplete logs are not included.

Table 5. Work: Home-Office Reaction to Stories
Percent

Characteristic of reporter	Number of responses	Amount of reaction		
		None	Occasional	Frequent
Employer				
Wire service	15	20.0	60.0	20.0
Network television	18	5.6	44.4	50.0
Radio	12	16.7	50.0	33.3
Specialized publication	22	22.7	31.8	45.5
Newspaper	66	13.6	51.5	34.8
Beat				
Congress	13	23.1	46.2	30.8
Diplomacy	12	8.3	41.7	50.0
Class A general assignment	8	12.5	0.0	87.5
Law	14	21.4	50.0	28.6
Economics	10	10.0	40.0	50.0
Regional	22	9.1	59.1	31.8
Domestic	11	27.3	54.5	18.2
Class B general assignment	23	21.7	43.5	34.8
Job satisfaction				
Very satisfied	56	14.3	37.5	48.2
Fairly satisfied	61	13.1	45.9	41.0
Somewhat dissatisfied	23	21.7	60.9	17.4
Assessment of own bureau				
Outstanding	14	14.3	35.7	50.0
Very good	46	19.6	30.4	50.0
Good	51	11.8	54.9	33.3
Fair	21	19.0	61.9	19.0
Total news corps	145	15.2	45.5	39.3

Table 6. Work: Travel on Assignment
Percent

Characteristic of reporter	Number of responses	Days out of Washington a year			
		None	One through fourteen	Fifteen through thirty	Over thirty
Male	131	35.1	22.9	18.3	23.7
Female	48	33.3	37.5	16.7	12.5
Age					
20–29	44	45.5	36.4	11.4	6.8
30–39	66	30.3	21.2	18.2	30.3
40–49	48	31.3	25.0	20.8	22.9
50 and over	21	33.3	28.6	23.8	14.3
Employer					
Wire service	16	37.5	43.8	18.8	0.0
Network television	19	15.8	5.3	26.3	52.6
Radio	18	38.9	22.2	5.6	33.3
Magazine	9	44.4	11.1	22.2	22.2
Specialized publication	35	48.6	40.0	8.6	2.9
Newspaper	73	28.8	24.7	24.7	21.9
Influential	62	29.0	17.7	24.2	29.0
Noninfluential	117	37.6	31.6	14.5	16.2
Beat					
White House	9	11.1	22.2	33.3	33.3
Congress	19	31.6	42.1	10.5	15.8
Diplomacy	18	5.6	16.7	33.3	44.4
Class A general assignment	12	25.0	8.3	8.3	58.3
Law	16	43.8	31.3	18.8	6.3
Economics	18	38.9	27.8	16.7	16.7
Energy	16	43.8	37.5	0.0	18.8
Regional	27	51.9	22.2	18.5	7.4
Domestic	26	30.8	23.1	19.2	26.9
Class B general assignment	28	42.9	28.6	14.3	14.3
Total news corps	179	34.6	26.8	17.9	20.7

Table 7. Work: Free-lancing

Characteristic of reporter	Number of responses	Percent responding yes
Male	378	27.5
Female	98	26.5
White	453	26.5
Black	17	52.9
Age		
20–29	99	25.3
30–39	180	23.9
40–49	119	31.9
50 and over	78	30.8
Employer		
Wire service	40	27.5
Network television	43	20.9
Radio	27	37.0
Magazine	33	21.2
Specialized publication	94	22.3
Newspaper	212	29.2
Influential	169	26.0
Noninfluential	301	27.9
Beat		
White House	29	31.0
Congress	42	33.3
Diplomacy	39	46.2
Class A general assignment	42	33.3
Law	28	21.4
Economics	41	19.5
Energy	20	25.0
Regional	79	19.0
Domestic	56	28.6
Class B general assignment	66	25.8
Politics	22	27.3
Total news corps	476	27.3

Table 8. Work: Job History
Percent

Item	Reporters
Number of jobs held in Washington	
One	74.7
Two	14.9
Three	5.7
Four	4.6
Number of respondents	(194)
Directions of job change	
Print to print	73.1
Broadcast to broadcast	17.9
Print to broadcast	5.1
Broadcast to print	3.8
Number of job changes	(78)

Table 9. Work: Washington News Corps' Isolation from Country
Percent

| Characteristic of reporter | Number of responses | Seriousness of isolation | | |
		A serious problem	A problem, not serious	Not a problem
Male	133	51.1	29.3	19.5
Female	46	63.0	23.9	13.0
Age				
20–29	44	47.7	29.5	22.7
30–39	64	62.5	28.1	9.4
40–49	50	52.0	26.0	22.0
50 and over	21	47.6	28.6	23.8
Employer				
Wire service	16	43.8	31.3	25.0
Network television	19	52.6	26.3	21.1
Radio	18	61.1	27.8	11.1
Magazine	9	33.3	44.4	22.2
Specialized publication	35	48.6	31.4	20.0
Newspaper	74	60.8	25.7	13.5
Influential	60	51.7	26.7	21.7
Noninfluential	119	55.5	28.6	16.0
Beat				
White House	8	87.5	12.5	0.0
Congress	15	40.0	26.7	33.3
Diplomacy	12	41.7	41.7	16.7
Class A general assignment	10	50.0	20.0	30.0
Law	13	53.8	23.1	23.1
Economics	15	66.7	20.0	13.3
Energy	11	45.5	18.2	36.4
Regional	26	50.0	38.5	11.5
Domestic	15	66.7	26.7	6.7
Class B general assignment	26	57.7	26.9	15.4
Specialist	64	53.1	28.1	18.8
Generalist	115	54.8	27.8	17.4
Travel (Days out of Washington per year)				
None	59	47.5	28.8	23.7
One through fourteen	45	55.6	31.1	13.3
Fifteen through thirty	31	51.6	25.8	22.6
Over thirty	35	60.0	28.6	11.4
Total news corps	179	54.2	27.9	17.9

Table 10. Work: Friendships among Washington Journalists

Characteristic of reporter	Number of responses	Average number of friendships with journalists[a]
Male	141	1.43
Female	53	1.28
Age		
20–29	49	1.27
30–39	70	1.33
40–49	53	1.42
50 and over	22	1.82
Employer		
Wire service	17	1.41
Network television	20	1.55
Radio	18	1.83
Magazine	11	1.18
Specialized publication	41	1.10
Newspaper	77	1.46
Influential	64	1.45
Noninfluential	130	1.36
Beat		
White House	8	1.63
Congress	15	1.73
Diplomacy	15	1.60
Class A general assignment	10	1.50
Law	15	1.33
Economics	16	1.00
Energy	13	1.23
Regional	27	1.52
Domestic	17	1.71
Class B general assignment	26	1.58
Total news corps	194	1.39

a. Reporters were asked how many of their three closest friends in Washington were journalists.

Table 11. News Organizations: Employment

Percent

			Employer			
Characteristic of reporter	Wire service	Network television	Radio	Magazine	Specialized publication	Newspaper
Male	90.0	81.4	77.8	78.8	67.0	84.9
Female	10.0	18.6	22.2	21.2	33.0	15.1
White	97.5	95.3	85.2	96.9	98.9	97.6
Black	2.5	4.7	14.8	3.1	1.1	2.4
Urban	66.7	76.3	64.0	71.0	70.0	74.2
Rural	25.0	15.8	20.0	16.1	27.8	22.2
Age						
20–29	15.0	2.3	51.9	12.1	29.8	15.1
30–39	40.0	39.5	25.9	36.4	39.4	40.1
40–49	17.5	39.5	22.2	15.2	19.1	30.2
50 and over	27.5	18.6	0.0	36.4	11.7	14.6
Regional influence						
Northeast	37.9	39.5	33.7	32.4	40.3	38.2
North Central	24.6	25.6	9.6	27.0	23.4	32.8
South	28.6	26.3	49.3	31.6	33.5	17.6
West	8.9	8.6	7.4	9.0	2.9	11.4
Education						
High school only	2.5	0.0	3.7	3.0	2.1	1.4
Some college	5.0	4.7	11.1	0.0	4.3	4.2
College degree	67.5	32.6	66.7	39.4	43.6	40.6

Table 11. (continued)
Percent

Characteristic of reporter	Employer					
	Wire service	Network television	Radio	Magazine	Specialized publication	Newspaper
Education (continued)						
Some graduate work	5.0	27.9	3.7	24.2	13.8	15.6
Graduate degree	20.0	34.9	14.8	33.3	36.2	38.2
Number of responses to each of above	(40)	(43)	(27)	(33)	(94)	(212)
College selectivity						
Highly selective	31.6	36.6	19.2	41.9	31.9	37.6
Selective	55.3	48.8	38.5	38.7	54.9	40.0
Not selective	13.2	14.6	42.3	19.4	13.2	22.4
Number of responses	(38)	(41)	(26)	(31)	(91)	(210)
Undergraduate field of study						
Humanities/liberal arts	51.4	57.5	34.6	48.4	58.9	59.3
Journalism	43.2	27.5	50.0	25.8	21.1	29.2
Science/technology	5.4	15.0	15.4	25.8	20.0	11.5
Number of undergraduate fields	(37)	(40)	(26)	(31)	(90)	(209)
Graduate field of study						
Humanities/liberal arts	22.2	37.5	...	30.8	28.3	23.6
Journalism	66.7	45.8	...	46.2	47.8	50.0
Science/technology	11.1	16.7	...	23.1	23.9	26.4
Number of graduate fields	(9)	(24)		(13)	(46)	(106)
Specialist	41.2	50.0	16.7	36.4	63.4	28.6
Generalist	58.8	50.0	83.3	63.6	36.6	71.4
Number of responses	(17)	(20)	(18)	(11)	(41)	(77)

Table 12. News Organizations: Employment Preferences[a]

Percent; figures in parentheses are number of responses

Characteristic of reporter	Possible employer							
	Wire service	Network television	Local television	Radio	Magazine	Specialized publication	Independent newspaper	Chain newspaper
Male	32.8 (128)	56.9 (130)	34.3 (134)	35.5 (124)	80.3 (132)	52.1 (121)	80.7 (119)	67.2 (122)
Female	32.7 (149)	56.0 (50)	46.2 (52)	40.0 (50)	82.4 (51)	37.5 (40)	78.3 (46)	56.0 (50)
Age								
20–29	45.7 (46)	61.2 (49)	44.9 (49)	40.9 (44)	91.7 (48)	45.9 (37)	77.6 (49)	56.5 (46)
30–39	30.3 (66)	59.7 (62)	42.4 (66)	36.1 (61)	81.8 (66)	49.2 (63)	82.7 (52)	64.1 (64)
40–49	22.9 (48)	54.2 (48)	33.3 (51)	33.3 (48)	74.0 (50)	44.4 (45)	81.8 (44)	74.4 (43)
50 and over	35.3 (17)	42.9 (21)	15.0 (20)	38.1 (21)	68.4 (19)	62.5 (16)	75.0 (20)	57.9 (19)
Employer								
Wire service	...	64.7 (17)	29.4 (17)	35.3 (17)	82.4 (17)	52.9 (17)	88.2 (17)	88.2 (17)
Network television	10.5 (19)	...	22.2 (18)	40.0 (15)	61.1 (18)	31.6 (19)	52.6 (19)	27.8 (18)
Radio	35.3 (17)	82.4 (17)	82.4 (17)	...	77.8 (18)	50.0 (18)	72.2 (18)	50.0 (18)
Magazine	10.0 (10)	50.0 (10)	20.0 (10)	20.0 (10)	...	50.0 (10)	90.0 (10)	50.0 (10)
Specialized publication	50.0 (40)	53.7 (41)	52.5 (40)	50.0 (40)	86.8 (38)	...	82.5 (40)	66.7 (39)
Newspaper	26.7 (75)	43.4 (76)	28.0 (75)	25.0 (76)	78.4 (74)	45.1 (71)	...	...
Total news corps	32.8 (177)	56.7 (180)	37.6 (186)	36.8 (174)	80.9 (183)	48.4 (161)	80.0 (165)	64.0 (172)

a. Reporters were asked whether they would work for each kind of news organization.

Table 13. **Beats: Reporters' Traits by Beat**
Percent

Characteristic of reporter	Beat										
	White House	Congress	Diplomacy	Class A general assignment	Law	Economics	Energy	Regional	Domestic	Class B general assignment	Politics
Male	86.2	83.3	97.4	90.5	67.9	80.5	75.0	83.5	62.5	74.2	95.5
Female	13.8	16.7	2.6	9.5	32.1	19.5	25.0	16.5	37.5	25.8	4.5
White	89.7	95.1	97.4	97.6	100.0	100.0	100.0	98.7	91.1	90.9	100.0
Black	10.3	4.9	2.6	2.4	0.0	0.0	0.0	1.3	8.9	9.1	0.0
Urban	65.4	64.9	75.7	72.5	70.4	79.5	84.2	75.0	68.5	86.4	66.7
Rural	34.6	27.0	13.5	22.5	25.9	17.9	10.5	19.4	22.2	10.2	33.3
Age											
20–29	6.9	16.7	5.1	7.1	7.1	26.8	20.0	32.9	21.4	30.3	4.5
30–39	58.6	42.9	33.3	33.3	50.0	43.9	30.0	31.6	48.2	33.3	36.4
40–49	17.2	19.0	43.6	33.3	21.4	17.1	40.0	19.0	12.5	22.7	54.5
50 and over	17.2	21.4	17.9	26.2	21.4	12.2	10.0	16.5	17.9	13.6	4.5
Regional influence											
Northeast	33.3	29.6	59.2	36.8	38.2	48.8	33.0	40.0	21.6	41.5	34.1
North Central	33.5	30.7	20.0	33.6	26.4	22.0	30.5	28.5	32.5	27.7	40.3
South	25.3	28.9	18.6	19.8	23.3	18.2	36.6	17.6	37.1	20.7	24.4
West	8.0	10.8	2.2	9.8	12.1	11.0	0.0	13.9	8.7	10.2	1.3
Education											
High school only	0.0	2.4	2.6	0.0	0.0	0.0	5.0	1.3	1.8	1.5	4.5
Some college	10.3	2.4	5.1	7.1	0.0	2.4	0.0	11.4	1.8	4.5	4.5

College degree	34.5	45.2	38.5	42.9	21.4	39.0	60.0	49.4	50.0	60.6	45.5
Some graduate work	13.8	21.4	17.9	14.3	14.3	12.2	10.0	13.9	21.4	13.6	18.2
Graduate degree	41.4	28.6	35.9	35.7	64.3	46.3	25.0	24.1	25.0	19.7	27.3
Number of responses to each of above	(29)	(42)	(39)	(42)	(28)	(41)	(20)	(79)	(56)	(66)	(22)
College selectivity											
Highly selective	27.6	38.5	50.0	29.3	32.1	43.9	15.8	27.6	25.5	36.9	45.5
Selective	44.8	46.2	39.5	51.2	53.6	43.9	78.9	43.4	45.5	44.6	40.9
Not selective	27.6	15.4	10.5	19.5	14.3	12.2	5.3	28.9	29.1	18.5	13.6
Number of responses	(29)	(39)	(38)	(41)	(28)	(41)	(19)	(76)	(55)	(65)	(22)
Undergraduate field of study											
Humanities/liberal arts	51.7	60.5	64.9	65.9	48.1	51.2	63.2	50.0	60.0	50.0	81.8
Journalism	41.4	31.6	29.7	14.6	37.0	19.5	36.8	38.2	23.6	34.4	13.6
Science/technology	6.9	7.9	5.4	19.5	14.8	29.3	0.0	11.8	16.4	15.6	4.5
Number of responses	(29)	(38)	(37)	(41)	(27)	(41)	(19)	(76)	(55)	(64)	(22)
Graduate field of study											
Humanities/liberal arts	33.3	41.2	33.3	31.6	5.3	13.6	⋮	25.0	25.0	25.0	60.0
Journalism	60.0	41.2	38.1	36.8	47.4	50.0	⋮	64.3	45.8	55.0	40.0
Science/technology	6.7	17.6	28.6	31.6	47.4	36.4	⋮	10.7	29.2	20.0	0.0
Number of responses	(15)	(17)	(21)	(19)	(19)	(22)	⋮	(28)	(24)	(20)	(10)
Specialist	37.5	26.7	73.3	20.0	53.3	50.0	53.8	14.8	64.7	3.8	⋮
Generalist	62.5	73.3	26.7	80.0	46.7	50.0	46.2	85.2	35.3	96.2	⋮
Number of responses	(8)	(15)	(15)	(10)	(15)	(16)	(13)	(27)	(17)	(26)	⋮

Table 14. Traits: Chain and Independent Newspapers
Percent

Characteristic of reporter	Employer	
	Chain newspaper	Independent newspaper
Male	87.9	83.8
Female	12.1	16.2
Urban	77.8	72.9
Rural	20.4	22.9
Regional influence		
Northeast	40.3	37.4
North Central	31.5	33.3
South	15.6	18.4
West	12.6	10.9
Education		
High school only	1.7	1.3
Some college	10.3	1.9
College degree	44.8	39.0
Some graduate work	13.8	16.2
Graduate degree	29.3	41.6
Number of responses to each of above	(58)	(154)
College selectivity		
Highly selective	39.3	37.0
Selective	32.1	42.9
Not selective	28.6	20.1
Number of responses	(56)	(154)
Undergraduate field of study		
Humanities/liberal arts	57.1	60.1
Journalism	33.9	27.5
Science/technology	8.9	12.4
Number of responses	(56)	(153)
Graduate field of study		
Humanities/liberal arts	15.0	31.4
Journalism	75.0	54.3
Science/technology	10.0	14.3
Number of responses	(20)	(70)

Table 15. Traits: Influential and Noninfluential News Organizations
Percent

	Employer	
Characteristic of reporter	Influential news organization	Noninfluential news organization
Male	84.0	76.7
Female	16.0	23.3
White	95.8	96.6
Black	4.2	3.4
Urban	70.3	74.0
Rural	21.9	22.1
Age		
20–29	7.7	27.6
30–39	43.2	35.5
40–49	28.4	22.9
50 and over	20.7	14.0
Regional influence		
Northeast	40.2	37.4
North Central	25.8	27.8
South	24.9	26.8
West	9.1	8.1
Education		
High school only	1.8	1.7
Some college	4.1	6.0
College degree	41.4	46.8
Some graduate work	17.2	14.0
Graduate degree	35.5	31.6
Number of responses to each of above	(169)	(301)
College selectivity		
Highly selective	39.3	31.4
Selective	42.3	47.8
Not selective	18.4	20.8
Number of responses	(163)	(293)
Undergraduate fields of study		
Humanities/liberal arts	67.1	58.1
Journalism	19.0	26.8
Science/technology	13.9	15.0
Number of undergraduate fields	(231)	(406)

Table 15 *(continued)*

	Employer	
Characteristic of reporter	*Influential news organization*	*Noninfluential news organization*
Graduate fields of study		
Humanities/liberal arts	33.7	27.7
Journalism	45.3	48.9
Science/technology	20.9	23.4
Number of graduate fields	(86)	(141)
Specialist	40.6	38.5
Generalist	59.4	61.5
Number of responses	(64)	(130)

Table 16. Traits: Age at Beginning of Washington News Career[a]
Percent

		Years of age			
Characteristic of reporter	*Number of responses*	*Under thirty*	*Thirty through thirty-nine*	*Forty through forty-nine*	*Fifty and over*
Male	141	49.6	39.0	9.9	1.4
Female	53	79.2	18.9	1.9	0.0
White	187	56.7	34.2	8.0	1.1
Black	7	85.7	14.3	0.0	0.0
Employer					
Wire service	17	35.3	52.9	5.9	5.9
Network television	20	25.0	60.0	15.0	0.0
Radio	18	83.3	11.1	5.6	0.0
Magazine	11	45.5	36.4	18.2	0.0
Specialized publication	41	65.9	29.3	4.9	0.0
Newspaper	77	59.7	32.5	6.5	1.3
Total news corps	194	57.7	33.5	7.7	1.0

a. Entry was mainly through home-office assignment (46.8 percent); others change jobs (31.4 percent); few entered Washington journalism with their first jobs (19.4 percent).

Table 17. Traits: Age
Percent

Characteristic of reporter	Twenty through twenty-nine	Thirty through thirty-nine	Forty through forty-nine	Fifty and over
Male	64.6	73.9	93.3	89.7
Female	35.4	26.1	6.7	10.3
White	90.9	96.1	100.0	98.7
Black	9.1	3.9	0.0	1.3
Urban	70.7	76.9	72.2	66.7
Rural	26.1	17.2	22.2	27.8
Employer				
Wire service	6.1	8.9	5.9	14.1
Network television	1.0	9.4	14.3	10.3
Radio	14.1	3.9	5.0	0.0
Magazine	4.0	6.7	4.2	15.4
Specialized publication	28.3	20.6	15.1	14.1
Newspaper	32.3	47.2	53.8	39.7
All other	14.2	2.4	1.6	6.4
Influential	13.5	40.6	41.0	45.5
Noninfluential	86.5	59.4	59.0	54.5
Beat				
White House	1.8	7.9	3.5	5.5
Congress	6.1	8.4	5.6	9.9
Diplomacy	1.8	6.0	11.9	7.7
Class A general assignment	2.6	6.5	9.8	12.1
Law	1.8	6.5	4.2	6.6
Economics	9.6	8.4	4.9	5.5
Energy	3.5	2.8	5.6	2.2
Regional	22.8	11.6	10.5	14.3
Domestic	10.5	12.6	4.9	11.0
Class B general assignment	17.5	10.2	10.5	9.9
Politics	0.9	3.7	8.4	1.1
All other	21.1	15.3	20.3	14.3
Regional influence				
Northeast	42.8	32.4	44.0	37.0
North Central	19.2	31.4	27.8	26.5
South	28.8	30.2	19.9	22.7
West	9.2	6.0	8.3	13.7

Table 17 *(continued)*

Characteristic of reporter	Years of age			
	Twenty through twenty-nine	*Thirty through thirty-nine*	*Forty through forty-nine*	*Fifty and over*
Education				
High school only	1.0	1.7	1.7	2.6
Some college	4.0	4.4	3.4	12.8
College degree	59.6	42.8	41.2	34.6
Some graduate work	16.2	15.6	15.1	14.1
Graduate degree	19.2	35.6	38.7	35.9
Number of responses to each of above	(99)	(180)	(119)	(78)
College selectivity				
Highly selective	37.8	27.7	41.7	36.1
Selective	42.9	53.1	38.3	41.7
Not selective	19.4	19.2	20.0	22.2
Number of responses	(98)	(177)	(115)	(72)
Undergraduate fields of study				
Humanities/liberal arts	55.2	61.4	67.7	59.6
Journalism	26.4	27.3	22.4	15.6
Science/technology	18.4	11.2	9.9	24.8
Number of undergraduate fields	(125)	(249)	(161)	(109)
Graduate fields of study				
Humanities/liberal arts	17.1	27.4	38.8	32.4
Journalism	51.4	53.7	40.3	41.2
Science/technology	31.4	18.9	20.9	26.5
Number of graduate fields	(35)	(95)	(67)	(34)
Specialist	36.7	37.1	35.8	59.1
Generalist	63.3	62.9	64.2	40.9
Number of responses	(49)	(70)	(53)	(22)

Table 18. Traits: Race and Sex
Percent

Characteristic of reporter	White	Black	Male	Female
Male	80.4	47.1	. . .	. . .
Female	19.6	52.9	. . .	. . .
Black	. . .	. . .	2.2	9.2
White	. . .	. . .	97.8	90.8
Urban	72.5	76.5	73.4	70.7
Rural	22.2	17.6	21.5	23.9
Employer				
Influential	35.8	37.5	38.1	27.8
Noninfluential	64.2	62.5	61.9	72.2
Regional influence				
Northeast	39.1	18.1	40.4	30.1
North Central	27.0	20.9	27.1	27.1
South	24.9	61.0	23.8	35.0
West	9.0	0.0	8.7	7.8
Education				
High school only	1.8	0.0	1.6	2.0
Some college	5.5	5.9	5.8	4.1
College degree	44.4	52.9	44.2	45.9
Some graduate work	15.2	11.8	13.2	23.5
Graduate degree	33.1	29.4	35.2	24.5
Number of responses to each of above	(453)	(17)	(372)	(98)
College selectivity				
Highly selective	35.3	11.8	37.2	25.0
Selective	46.0	35.3	44.0	51.0
Not selective	18.7	52.9	18.9	24.0
Number of responses	(439)	(17)	(366)	(96)
Undergraduate fields of study				
Humanities/liberal arts	62.4	36.4	63.3	54.8
Journalism	23.2	40.9	22.4	29.6
Science/technology	14.4	22.7	14.3	15.6
Number of undergraduate fields	(611)	(22)	(509)	(135)

Table 18 *(continued)*
Percent

Characteristic of reporter	White	Black	Male	Female
Graduate fields of study				
Humanities/liberal arts	30.5	0.0	31.4	23.3
Journalism	46.8	83.3	46.3	53.5
Science/technology	22.7	16.7	22.3	23.3
Number of graduate fields	(220)	(6)	(188)	(43)
Specialist	39.6	28.6	38.3	41.5
Generalist	60.4	71.4	61.7	58.5
Number of responses	(187)	(7)	(141)	(53)

Table 19. Traits: Washington Reporters and U.S. Population, by Sex, Race, and Age
Percent

Characteristic of reporter	Washington reporters (1978)	United States	
		Journalists (1971)	Professional population (1978)
Male	79.4	79.7	66.4
Female	20.6	20.3	33.6
White	96.4	n.a.	91.3
Black	3.6	3.9	8.7
Age			
20–29	20.8	32.4	31.4
30–39	37.8	23.9	24.0
40–49	25.0	21.1	19.1
50 and over	16.4	21.8	25.6

Sources: Data for U.S. journalists from John W. C. Johnstone, Edward J. Slawski, and William W. Bowman, *The News People* (University of Illinois Press, 1976), pp. 197, 198. The data do not indicate what percentage of the nonblack journalist population is white. Data for professional U.S. population from Bureau of Labor Statistics, *Employment and Earnings*, vol. 25 (GPO, August 1978), pp. 21, 34, 35.
n.a. Not available.

Table 20. Traits: Washington Reporters and U.S. Population, by Education and Region
Percent

Characteristic of reporter	Washington reporters (1978)	United States	
		Journalists (1971)	Total population (1975, education; 1978, region)
Education			
Some college	98.3	86.1	30.4
College degree	92.8	58.2	21.4
Some graduate work	48.3	18.6	5.7
Graduate degree	33.0	8.1	1.5
Region			
Northeast	38.3	n.a.	23.0
North Central	27.1	n.a.	26.6
South	26.1	n.a.	32.3
West	8.5	n.a.	18.1

Sources: Data for U.S. journalists from Johnstone, Slawski, and Bowman, *The News People*, p. 200. Estimates for education of total population are based on Douglas L. Adkins, *The Great American Degree Machine* (Berkeley: Carnegie Foundation for the Advancement of Teaching, 1975), table 6.4; regional population data for total population are from the U.S. Bureau of the Census, *Current Population Reports*, series P-20, no. 331, "Geographical Mobility: March 1975 to March 1978" (GPO, 1978), p. 7.

Table 21. Traits: Fields of Study
Percent

Subject	Reporters
Undergraduate	
Humanities/liberal arts	61.5
Journalism	23.9
Science/technology	14.6
Number of undergraduate fields	(644)
Graduate	
Humanities/liberal arts	29.9
Journalism	47.6
Science/technology	22.5
Number of graduate fields	(231)
Undergraduate and graduate	
Humanities/liberal arts only	33.1
Humanities/liberal arts + journalism	24.7
Journalism only	15.6
Humanities/liberal arts + science/technology	10.2
Science/technology only	7.4
Science/technology + journalism	5.6
Humanities/liberal arts + journalism + science/technology	3.5
Number of undergraduate and graduate fields	(875)

Table 22. Impressions: Reporters' Opinions on Professional Questions
Percent

Item	Reporters
Pack journalism	
Serious problem	56.8
Problem, not serious	35.5
Not a problem	7.7
Number of responses	(183)
Personalities journalism	
Serious problem	28.6
Problem, not serious	27.5
Not a problem	44.0
Number of responses	(182)
Duplication of coverage	
Serious problem	33.0
Problem, not serious	25.4
Not a problem	41.6
Number of responses	(185)
Is duplication encouraged by editors?	
Yes	64.2
No	35.8
Number of responses	(120)
Lack of coverage of regulatory agencies	
Serious problem	50.6
Problem, not serious	33.9
Not a problem	15.6
Number of responses	(180)
Does public gain from backgrounders?[a]	
Gains	71.0
Loses	16.9
Gains and loses	9.3
Neither gains nor loses	2.7
Number of responses	(183)
Do reporters make it too easy for sources to go on background?[a]	
Yes	67.4
No	32.6
Number of responses	(175)
Is too much time spent on breaking news?	
Serious problem	24.9
Problem, not serious	25.4
Not a problem	49.7
Number of responses	(169)

Table 22 *(continued)*

Item	Reporters
Is there need for more research help?	
Yes	34.1
Some	17.9
No	48.0
Number of responses	(173)
Are reporters out-of-touch with the nation?	
Serious problem	54.2
Problem, not serious	27.9
Not a problem	17.9
Number of responses	(179)
Should reporters spend more time away from Washington?	
Yes	80.9
No	19.1
Number of responses	(157)
Should there be more rotation between Washington and other assignment locations?	
Yes	52.3
No	47.7
Number of responses	(153)
If there was a strict rotation policy, would your organization lose reporters?	
Yes	61.6
No	38.4
Number of responses	(125)
Is there work other than journalism you would like to do someday?	
Yes	50.5
No	49.5
Number of responses	(184)

a. "Background" allows the reporters to use information without identifying its source.

Table 23. Newspapers Surveyed[a]

Newspaper and state	Daily circulation (1977)	Time of distribution (1978)
Anniston Star (Alabama)	27,800	P.M.
Atlanta Constitution (Georgia)	207,589	A.M.
Baltimore News American (Maryland)	175,933	P.M.
Boston Globe (Massachusetts)	291,073	A.M./P.M.
Burlington Free Press (Vermont)	45,913	A.M.
Chicago Tribune (Illinois)	746,069	A.M.
Columbus Dispatch (Ohio)	194,525	P.M.
Dallas Morning News (Texas)	260,249	A.M.
Denver Post (Colorado)	250,929	P.M.
Des Moines Register (Iowa)	225,094	A.M.
Greensburg Tribune-Review (Pennsylvania)	38,826	A.M./P.M.
Los Angeles Times (California)	1,008,995	A.M.
Milwaukee Journal (Wisconsin)	338,597	P.M.
New Orleans Times-Picayune (Louisiana)	208,354	A.M.
New York Daily News (New York)	1,925,643	A.M.
New York Times (New York)	803,123	A.M.
Philadelphia Inquirer (Pennsylvania)	421,627	A.M.
Pittsburgh Press (Pennsylvania)	259,270	P.M.
Richmond News Leader (Virginia)	112,807	P.M.
San Diego Union (California)	182,700	A.M.
Seattle Times (Washington)	224,404	P.M.
Washington Post (District of Columbia)	530,031	A.M.

a. Washington dateline news stories about national government were coded for April 9–15, 1978. The *Richmond News Leader* does not have a Sunday edition. Regional news from the *Washington Post* was not coded. Newspaper chains represented: Copley (*San Diego Union*), Cox (*Atlanta Constitution*), Gannett (*Burlington Free Press*), Hearst (*Baltimore News American*), Knight-Ridder (*Philadelphia Inquirer*), Media General (*Richmond News Leader*), Newhouse (*New Orleans Times-Picayune*), Scripps-Howard (*Pittsburgh Press*).

Index

Aberbach, Joel D., 101n
Adams, John Quincy, 102
Adler, Richard, 31n
Administrative work. *See* Office work
Age groups: beat characteristics, 49–50, 65, 76, 77; career patterns, 127–29; fifties and above, 79–82; forties, 78–79; job satisfaction, 3, 33; news-organization characteristics, 30, 33, 34, 39, 74, 77, 79, 80; reporter characteristics, 67–68, 73–82, 85–86, 90; thirties, 76–78; twenties, 74–76; work characteristics, 3, 8, 10, 12, 13, 17
Agronsky, Martin, 30n
Alsop, Stewart, 49
American Broadcasting Company, 24n, 29. *See also* Television
American Society of Newspaper Editors, 72
Anniston Star, 92n, 96
Appel, Kevin R., 105
Argyris, Chris, 22n
Associated Press, 2n, 24n, 35, 60, 77, 93, 132. *See also* Wire services
Atlanta Constitution, 26n, 37
Atlanta Journal, 26n, 37
Atlantic, 26n, 43, 83n
Attribution, 19–20, 56, 57
Autonomy: beat characteristics, 9, 51, 66; characteristics of, 133–37; news-organization characteristics, 37–38, 41; work characteristics, 3–8, 20

Babb, Laura Longley, 119n
Background interviews. *See* Attribution
Bagdikian, Ben H., 38, 61n, 83n
Baker, Howard, 102
Baker, Russell, 53–54
Baltimore News American, 114
Baltimore Sun, 26, 27
Balutis, Alan P., 97, 98n
Beats: autonomy, 9, 51, 66; desirability, 18, 49–52; educational characteristics, 52–55,

59; geographical, 47; job satisfaction, 2; news-organization characteristics, 32, 40; organizational change and, 50; reporter characteristics, 69, 70, 72–73, 76, 77, 79, 84, 86; reporter distribution, 48–49; specialization, 63–66; story characteristics, 109–10; substantive, 47–48; work characteristics, 2, 6–11, 13, 15–16, 18–19, 22
Beavan, John, 136n
Berkeley Barb, 118
Bernstein, Carl, 20n, 29, 127
Birnbaum, Max, 83n
Blacks: beat characteristics, 65, 72–73; job satisfaction, 33; news-organization characteristics, 33, 72, 90; reporter characteristics, 71–74, 86; work characteristics, 6, 13
Blanchard, Robert O., 48n
Bogart, Leo, 4n
Boston Globe, 26, 43
Bowman, William W., 84n
Boyd, Robert S., 47
Bradlee, Ben, 20n
Braestrup, Peter, 40n
Bray, Howard, 42n
Breaking news, 15–16, 121–23
Breed, Warren, 6n, 124
Brinkley, David, 31
Broadcast journalism. *See* Radio; Television
Broder, David S., 51n, 75, 123
Broh, C. Anthony, 123n
Bryan, William Jennings, 63
Brzezinski, Zbigniew, 60
Buffalo News, 92n, 97n
Burby, John F., 65n
Bureau chiefs: age characteristics, 78, 80–81; office work, 42–43; supervision, 6–8, 39, 73–74
Bureau of National Affairs, 34
Business Week, 64
Byrd, Harry F., Jr., 102n
Byrne, John A., 61n